Lecture Notes in Computer Science   13012

More information about this subseries at http://www.springer.com/series/7408

Iris Reinhartz-Berger · Shazia Sadiq (Eds.)

Advances in Conceptual Modeling

ER 2021 Workshops CoMoNoS, EmpER, CMLS
St. John's, NL, Canada, October 18–21, 2021
Proceedings

 Springer

Editors
Iris Reinhartz-Berger 🄳
University of Haifa
Haifa, Israel

Shazia Sadiq 🄳
The University of Queensland
Brisbane, QLD, Australia

ISSN 0302-9743   ISSN 1611-3349 (electronic)
Lecture Notes in Computer Science
ISBN 978-3-030-88357-7   ISBN 978-3-030-88358-4 (eBook)
https://doi.org/10.1007/978-3-030-88358-4

LNCS Sublibrary: SL2 – Programming and Software Engineering

This Springer imprint is published by the registered company Springer Nature Switzerland AG
The registered company address is: Gewerbestrasse 11, 6330 Cham, Switzerland

Preface

As we all grapple with the uncertainties and disruptions of the global COVID-19 pandemic, the ability to present complex phenomena in understandable and accessible representations is more important than ever, highlighting the important role that the conceptual modeling community can play in this regard. The ER conference has a proud and enduring history of advancing the body of knowledge in conceptual modeling. Now in its 40th edition, the ER 2021 general chairs Jeff Parsons and Joerge Evermann together with the program chairs, Aditya Chose, Jennifer Horkoff and Vitor E. Silva Souza, have assembled an impressive program in spite of the difficulties in conference organization. This includes a number of satellite events held in conjunction with the main conference.

ER workshops have continued to serve as an intensive collaborative forum for exchanging innovative ideas about conceptual modeling, and for discovering new frontiers for its use. This year we specifically invited proposals for interactive workshops on new, emerging, or established topics in conceptual modeling, or its application in specific domains. In spite of the challenges posed by the pandemic, five workshops were organized. This volume contains the proceedings of three of them.

CoMoNoS 2021, the 2nd Workshop on Conceptual Modeling for NoSQL Data Stores, was organized by Meike Klettke, Stefanie Scherzinger, and Uta Störl. In designing an application backed by a NoSQL data store, developers face specific challenges that match the strengths of the ER community, and hence the objective of CoMoNoS is to explore opportunities for conceptual modeling, addressing real-world problems that arise with NoSQL data stores (like MongoDB, Couchbase, Cassandra, or Neo4j). Four papers were presented at CoMoNoS 2021 and are included in these proceedings.

Dominik Bork, Miguel Goulao, Joao Araujo, and Sotirios Liaskos have continued to grow the International Workshop on Empirical Methods in Conceptual Modeling, this year in its 4th edition (EmpER 2021). This workshop aims at bringing together researchers and practitioners with an interest in the empirical investigation of conceptual modeling systems and practices. The workshop invites reports on specific finished, on-going, or proposed empirical studies, as well as theoretical, review, and experience papers about empirical research in conceptual modeling. The three papers presented at EmpER 2021 and included in these proceedings demonstrate the diversity of studies within empirical methods in conceptual modelling.

The objective of CMLS 2021, the 2nd Workshop on Conceptual Modeling for Life Sciences, organized by Anna Bernasconi, Arif Canakoglu, Ana León, and José Fabián Reyes Román, was to be a meeting point for information systems (IS), conceptual modeling (CM), and data management (DM) researchers working on healthcare and life science problems, and an opportunity to share, discuss and find new approaches to improve promising fields, with a special focus on genomic data management and precision medicine. Four papers were presented at CMLS 2021 and are included here.

Besides the above three workshops, we had two additional workshops at ER 2021. The organizers of CMAI 2021, the 3rd International Workshop on Conceptual Modeling meets AI, Dominik Bork, Peter Fettke, Ulrich Reimer, and Marina Tropmann-Frick, stipulate that the approaches to conceptual modeling as well as earlier approaches to AI have mainly focused on the manual engineering of models, requiring a great deal of time and money, with poor results in terms of scalability. They designed this workshop with the aim of exploring the huge potential in combining manual model engineering with data-driven artificial intelligence techniques. CMAI 2021 was conducted as a discussion-oriented workshop with invited contributions, recently published elsewhere, on the intersection of CM and AI. Several key researchers reported on their particular experiences in this area.

Finally, i* 2021, the 14th International i* Workshop, organized by Tong Li, Vik Pant, and Marcela Ruiz, aimed to provide a platform for the conceptual modeling community to exchange the latest ideas and research on goal modeling. The workshop accepted 10 papers that were presented at the ER 2021 and published with CEUR Workshop Proceedings.

We would like to thank all the workshop organizers for the organization of the workshops, and for assembling an impressive program of papers and presentations. We acknowledge the critical role of satellite events in major international conferences such as ER 2021 and the significant value they add for the community, in particular to seed new ideas, open new avenues and directions for research, and provide a forum for scientific exchange. We are also grateful to the authors and all reviewers involved in the ER 2021 workshops, for ensuring the high quality of the workshop program. Finally, we would like to extend our thanks to the general chairs of ER 2021, Jeff Parsons and Joerge Everman, for their continuous support and to Springer's assistant editor Anna Kramer for her guidance and help during the preparation of the proceedings.

October 2021   Iris Reinhartz-Berger
Shazia Sadiq

ER 2021 Conference Organization

General Chairs

Jeff Parsons   Memorial University of Newfoundland, Canada
Joerg Evermann   Memorial University of Newfoundland, Canada

Program Committee Chairs

Aditya Ghose   University of Wollongong, Australia
Jennifer Horkoff   University of Gothenburg, Sweden
Vítor E. Silva Souza   Federal University of Espírito Santo, Brazil

Workshop Chairs

Iris Reinhartz-Berger   University of Haifa, Israel
Shazia Sadiq   The University of Queensland, Australia

Tutorial Chairs

Wolfgang Maass   DFKI, Germany
Shuigeng Zhou   Fudan University, China

Poster and Demo Chairs

Roman Lukyanenko   HEC Montréal, Canada
Binny Samuel   University of Cincinnati, USA
Arnon Sturm   Ben-Gurion University, Israel

Panel Chairs

Sudha Ram   University of Arizona, USA
Il-Yeol Song   Drexel University, USA

Doctoral Consortium Chairs

Veda Storey   Georgia State University, USA
Carson Woo   University of British Columbia, Canada

Publicity Chairs

Arturo Castellanos   Baruch College, USA
Renuka Sindhgatta   Queensland University of Technology, Australia

Steering Committee Liasion

Erik Yu   University of Toronto, Canada

ER 2021 Workshop Organization

Conceptual Modeling for NoSQL Data Stores (CoMoNoS) 2021 Co-chairs

Meike Klettke   University of Rostock, Germany
Stefanie Scherzinger   University of Passau, Germany
Uta Störl   Darmstadt University of Applied Sciences, Germany

Empirical Methods in Conceptual Modeling (EmpER) 2021 Co-chairs

Dominik Bork   TU Wien, Austria
Miguel Goulão   Universidade NOVA de Lisboa, Portugal
João Araujo   Universidade NOVA de Lisboa, Portugal
Sotirios Liaskos   York University, Canada

Conceptual Modeling for Life Sciences (CMLS) 2021 Co-chairs

Anna Bernasconi   Politecnico di Milano, Italy
Arif Canakoglu   Politecnico di Milano, Italy
Ana León Palacio   Universitat Politécnica de Valéncia, Spain
José Fabián Reyes Roman   Universitat Politécnica de Valéncia, Spain

ER 2021 Workshop Program Committees

CoMoNoS 2021 Program Committee

Md.-A. Baazizi	Sorbonne University, France
Angela Bonifati	University of Lyon, France
Dario Colazzo	Paris Dauphine University, France
I. Comyn-Wattiau	ESSEC Business School, France
E. C. de Almeida	Federal University of Paraná, Brazil
Jesús García Molina	University of Murcia, Spain
Sven Hartmann	University of Clausthal, Germany
Irena Holubova	Charles University, Czech Republic
Jiaheng Lu	University of Helsinki, Finland
Michael Mior	Rochester Institute of Technology, USA
Norbert Ritter	University of Hamburg, Germany
Diego Sevilla Ruiz	University of Murcia, Spain
Carlo Sartiani	University of Pisa, Italy
Johannes Schildgen	OTH Regensburg, Germany
Heiko Schuldt	University of Basel, Switzerland
Lena Wiese	Fraunhofer Institute ITEM Hannover, Germany
Wolfram Wingerath	Baqend, Germany

EmpER 2020 Program Committee

Silvia Abrahao	Universidad Politécnica de Valencia, Spain
Nelly Condori-Fernández	Universidade da Coruña, Spain
Marian Daun	Universität Duisburg-Essen, Germany
Robson Fidalgo	Federal University of Pernambuco, Brazil
Sepideh Ghanavati	University of Maine, USA
Catarina Gralha	Universidade NOVA de Lisboa, Portugal
Alicia Grubb	Smith College, Canada
Katsiaryna Labunets	TU Delft, The Netherlands
Tong Li	Beijing University of Technology, Japan
Lin Liu	Tsinghua University, China
Jan Mendling	Humboldt-Universität zu Berlin, Germany
Oscar Pastor	Universidad Politécnica de Valencia, Spain
Geert Poels	Ghent University, Belgium
Iris Reinhartz-Berger	University of Haifa, Israel
Ben Roelens	Open University of the Netherlands, The Netherlands
Carla Silva	Universidade Federal de Pernambuco, Brazil
Manuel Wimmer	Johannes Kepler University Linz, Austria

CMLS 2021 Program Committee

Giuseppe Agapito	Università Magna Graecia di Catanzaro, Italy
Raffaele Calogero	Università di Torino, Italy
Mario Cannataro	Università Magna Graecia di Catanzaro, Italy
Matteo Chiara	Università di Milano, Italy
Johann Eder	Alpen-Adria University Klagenfurt, Austria
Jose Luis Garrido	University of Granada, Spain
Giancarlo Guizzardi	Free University of Bozen-Bolzano, Italy
Carlos Íñiguez-Jarrín	Escuela Politècnica Nacional, Ecuador
Sergio Lifschitz	Pontifícia Universidade Católica do Rio de Janeiro, Brazil
Paolo Missier	Newcastle University, UK
Ignacio Panach	University of Valencia, Spain
Barbara Pernici	Politecnico di Milano, Italy
Pietro Pinoli	Politecnico di Milano, Italy
Rosario Michael Piro	Politecnico di Milano, Italy
Sudha Ram	University of Arizona, US
Maria Rodriguez	IBM Zürich Research Laboratory, Switzerland, Martinez

Contents

Conceptual Modeling for NoSQL Data Stores (CoMoNoS) 2021

CoMoNoS 2021 Preface

The objective of the 2nd Workshop on Conceptual Modeling for NoSQL Data Stores (CoMoNoS) is to explore opportunities for applying conceptual modeling techniques to real-world problems that arise with NoSQL data stores (such as MongoDB, Couchbase, Cassandra, or Neo4J). In designing an application backed by a NoSQL data store, developers face specific challenges that match the strengths of the ER community. The purpose of this workshop is to grow a community of researchers and industry practitioners working on conceptual modeling for NoSQL data stores. The workshop provides a forum for researchers to learn about the actual pain points faced by practitioners. Equally, it is our aim that practitioners benefit from the experience of the ER research community at large, and the authors of the workshop articles in particular.

Among seven submissions, the Program Committee selected four research articles (three long papers and one short paper). Main topics of the workshop were schema reverse engineering methods, requirements engineering in NoSQL schema design, managing NoSQL schema evolution, schema mappings, and dedicated schema definition languages.

An invited industry keynote by Hannes Voigt from Neo4J covered the current state in the standardization of graph query languages.

Acknowledgments. We would like to thank the members of our Program Committee. This workshop was further supported by the Deutsche Forschungsgemeinschaft (DFG, German Research Foundation), grant #385808805.

October 2021

Meike Klettke
Stefanie Scherzinger
Uta Störl

Mapping Multidimensional Schemas to Property Graph Models

Jacky Akoka[1,2], Isabelle Comyn-Wattiau[3]([✉]), Cédric du Mouza[1], and Nicolas Prat[3]

[1] CEDRIC-CNAM, Paris, France
{akoka,dumouza}@cnam.fr
[2] Institut Mines Telecom-Business School, Evry, France
[3] ESSEC Business School, Cergy, France
{wattiau,prat}@essec.edu

Abstract. Multidimensional data warehouses represent an important artefact used by organizations to facilitate decision-making. However, they can be inefficient to cope with the growing need to execute complex queries. In addition, they experience difficulties in managing sparse matrices and are not efficient in managing schemas' evolution. To deal with these problems, we propose to transform these multidimensional models into NoSQL graph models. Our approach ensures the automatic mapping of multidimensional schemas into property graph models. It consists of a set of mapping rules defined between two meta-models, namely multidimensional and property graph meta models. Finally, we illustrate the application of our approach to a case study and discuss its validation.

Keywords: Multidimensional schema · Graph model · Meta-model · Mapping rules

1 Introduction

Nowadays, organizations must cope with growing data volume, data variety, and a greater complexity of their business environment. Decision-making, in this context, requires online analytical processing (OLAP) tools based on multidimensional data warehouses. They benefit from the advantages of the relational model, such as simple data model, low data redundancy, high data consistency, and a uniform query language [19].

However, the supremacy of the relational and the multidimensional models are challenged by NoSQL databases, and not only for performance reasons. NoSQL databases, and particularly graph databases, are becoming one solution to cope with several multidimensional data warehouse issues. The first issue is related to the inefficiency, even their impossibility, when executing certain complex queries. For some categories of queries, graph databases are very efficient [3]. The second issue lies in the management of sparse matrices frequent in multidimensional models [15]. The third issue stems from the difficulty of dealing with schema evolution [4]. Finally, analyzing multidimensional data from multiple perspectives and granularities remains complex [2].

© Springer Nature Switzerland AG 2021
I. Reinhartz-Berger and S. Sadiq (Eds.): ER 2021 Workshops, LNCS 13012, pp. 3–14, 2021.
https://doi.org/10.1007/978-3-030-88358-4_1

Due to the problems described above, we may use NoSQL graph databases to express a growing number of business intelligence (BI) applications in terms of nodes and edges. They are particularly useful when the focus is the relationships between the data. Moreover, they offer a visual representation, to support decision-making.

The aim of this paper is to propose a set of rules enabling the automatic mapping of multidimensional data warehouses schemas to NoSQL graph schemas, capitalizing on two existing meta-models, namely multidimensional [16] and property graph meta models [10]. We illustrate the application of our approach to a case study.

The rest of this paper is organized as follows. In Sect. 2, we present a state of the art on transformation approaches of multidimensional data warehouses to NoSQL databases. In Sect. 3, we present a motivating example, the instantiation of the source multidimensional meta-model, and the target graph meta-model. In Sect. 4, we describe the mapping rules allowing us to transform a multidimensional schema to a NoSQL graph schema and we illustrate it using the motivating example. Section 5 focuses on the validation. We present the conclusion and future research in Sect. 6.

2   Related Work

There are a few papers focusing on transforming multidimensional data warehouses schemas to NoSQL databases schemas. Some authors propose transformation rules of multidimensional models into column-oriented NoSQL models [5, 7, 11]. Regarding document-oriented approaches, several approaches have been proposed [8, 9, 20]. Document as well as column databases are very performant in many situations but do not cope efficiently with complex relations between data.

Regarding graph-oriented approach, Castelltort [6] proposes an approach transforming facts into nodes. The measures associated with each fact are stored as properties in the same node. The dimensions are also transformed into nodes. Relationships between nodes link facts to dimensions as well as attributes of dimensions to each other. Sellami [18] proposes rules for transforming a multidimensional conceptual model into a NoSQL graph-oriented model. Each fact and dimension parameters are transformed into nodes. Every dimension identifier is transformed into one node. However, they do not fully exploit the graph capabilities since measures are contained in properties of the nodes representing the facts. Moreover, their transformation rules imply complete redundancies of dimension hierarchies. On the contrary, Castelltort [6] allows graphs to share parts of common hierarchies, thus dealing with multiple hierarchies. However, they do not consider non-strict hierarchies and do not address the transformation of conceptual multidimensional models.

The research gap we address lies in the conceptual consideration of all the specificities of hierarchies, not only multiple, but also non-strict and/or reflexive. In the same way, we consider complex problems of fact dimensioning. Let us point out that the objective is not to deal with scalability issues. From a performance point of view, graph databases are neither appropriate nor optimized for OLAP analytical queries that process large batches of data with regular schema [11, 12]. Our objective is to tackle the problem of mapping multidimensional schemas to graph schemas at the *logical level*.

3 Motivating Example, Meta-models, and Instantiation

In this section, we successively describe the motivating example, the source multidimensional meta model and its instantiation, and the target graph meta model.

3.1 Motivating Example

We consider past advertising campaigns in a company. A campaign is launched for a product, starts on a certain day, and is published in one or several media (non-strict dimensioning). The campaign has a duration (measured in days), a cost and results in a sales increase, measured in volume. The latter represents the extra sales of the product, in quantity, that results from the advertising campaign. The cost of a campaign is imputed to the different media based on a coefficient. Similarly, the sales increase is attributed to the different media based on a coefficient (the imputation rule is not necessarily the same as for cost). The other fact class stores the sales by product and by date, expressed both in volume and in turnover (amount).

3.2 Source Multidimensional Meta-model and Instantiation

We present in Fig. 1 the UML class diagram of the meta-model proposed in [16].

For space reasons, we do not describe this meta-model since it has been the subject of the referenced article. Instead, we present its instantiation to the motivating example (Fig. 2). The notation uses UML stereotypes. The fact *Campaign* is dimensioned by the dimensions *Media, Product and Time*. Facts are composed of measures. Dimensions are composed of hierarchies. For example, the measures *duration, cost,* and *sales_increase_in_volume* characterize the fact *Campaign*. The hierarchies *Media → Media_type → All* and *Day → Month → Year → All* respectively compose the dimensions *Media* and *Time* whereas the dimension *Product* has two hierarchies: *Product → Sub_category → Category → All* and *Product → Category → All*, since some products have no subcategory and are related directly to their category. Moreover, the hierarchy of subcategories is reflexive. Hierarchies are made of successive rollup relationships between dimension levels (e.g. the hierarchy *Media → Media_type → All* has three dimension levels, linked by rollup relationships). A hierarchy is an aggregation path between successive dimension levels.

For a given measure in a n-dimensional (hyper)cube, a combination of n coordinates of dimension members, instances of dimension levels, e.g. *("Channel 1", "Mini32", 2009-01-01),* uniquely identifies a cell and therefore a measure value *(duration of 20 days, cost of 200 K€, sales increase of 150 units).* The roles of rollup relationships are characterized by their multiplicity. For example, when the lower multiplicity of the source role is *0*, we have an asymmetric hierarchy or "drill-down incomplete" hierarchy. In the hierarchy *Product → Sub_category → Category → All*, since some categories are not subdivided into sub-categories, we have an asymmetric hierarchy. When the upper multiplicity of the target role of a rollup is * (i.e. the target is plural), we have a non-strict hierarchy which may require the definition of a coefficient. In our example, in the hierarchy *Product → Category → All*, we assume that each product belongs to exactly one category. The lower multiplicity of the target role is *0* in case of

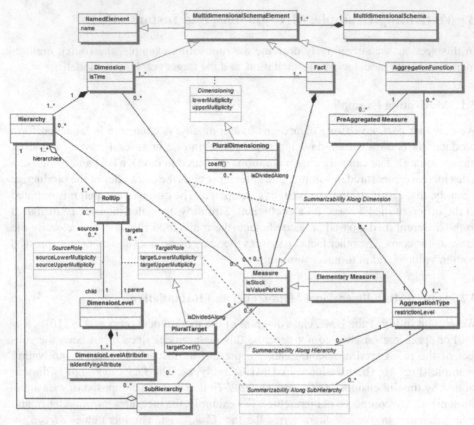

Fig. 1. The conceptual multidimensional meta-model [16]

"rollup incomplete" hierarchy. For example, in the hierarchy *Product* → *Sub_category* → *Category* → *All,* some products may not be attached to a sub-category.

We also consider unusual fact-dimension relationship (called dimensionings in our model). As for rollups, a dimensioning may be non-strict (plural) or incomplete. Non-strict (plural) dimensionings may require the definition of a coefficient. As an illustration, we assume that an advertising campaign may be launched in several media simultaneously. In this case, the dimensioning between *Media* and *Campaign* is plural. The cost of an advertising campaign is imputed to the different media based on a coefficient. Similarly, the sales increase is attributed to the different media based on a coefficient.

The metamodel enables the data warehouse designer to specify applicable aggregation functions for the different measures. The applicable aggregation functions (SUM, AVG, MIN, MAX, and COUNT) may be specified for a measure along a dimension, along a specific hierarchy, or along a subhierarchy (not represented on the diagram for space reasons). In the case of sales increase in volume, it does not make sense to compare together quantities of different subcategories of product; therefore, starting from *Sub_category,* only COUNT is applicable to this measure. Therefore, for the measure *sales_increase_in_volume,* we distinguish between two sub-hierarchies for the product:

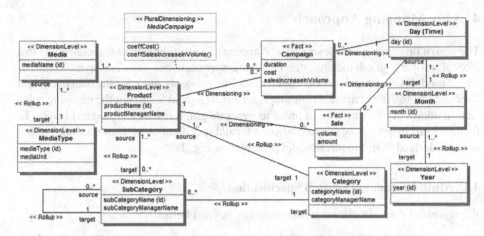

Fig. 2. Media-planning example: conceptual multidimensional schema

the sub-hierarchy *Product → Sub_category* and the sub-hierarchy *Sub_category → Category → All.* In summary, to explicitly illustrate the advantages that our approach has over the previous work (see Sect. 2), our case study tackles the issues of redundancy in dimensions, includes multiple measures, and appropriately handles hierarchies.

3.3 Property Graph Meta-model

The graph meta-model [10] comprises a set of *nodes* and a set of *edges*. Each *node* has a *label*, a *property* named "type", a *set of outgoing edges*, a *set of incoming edges*, and a *collection of properties*. Each *edge* has a *label*, an *outgoing tail node*, an *incoming head node*, a *label*, and a *collection of properties*. We propose to use the labels (node labels as well as edge labels) to structure the graph. Borrowing from [10], we derive the following specification: A graph database is defined as a tuple *GDB = (NO; ED; PR)*, where *NO* is the set of node definitions, and *ED* the set of edge definitions, and *PR* the set of property definitions that compose the graph. We use this specification below for the description of the mapping rules.

4   Our Mapping Approach

The aim of this section is to describe the mapping of a multidimensional meta-model to a NoSQL property-graph meta-model. Using this approach, one can develop multidimensional models using standard conceptual modeling concepts and store the data in a graph database. Note that we are deriving graph schemas (logical level) but the mapping rules can, in addition, be completed in order to generate graph instances (physical level). To facilitate this mapping, we propose below a formal specification of the multidimensional schema derived from the meta-model presented at Fig. 1.

4.1   Multidimensional Schema Specification

We represent the main classes of the model as defined below:

$DL = \{dl_1, dl_2, .., dl_n\}$ a set of dimension levels where each dl_i is a dimension level name. In the same way, let $D, A, M, F, H, SH, R, TR, DI, AF, AT$ be a set of respectively dimensions, dimension level attributes, measures, facts, hierarchies, subhierarchies, rollups, target roles, dimensionings, aggregation functions, and aggregation types.

We define below the main relations with mathematical functions between sets:

- *composed_of*: $H \rightarrow D$ where *composed_of(h_i)=d_j* if d_j is the basic dimension level of the h_i hierarchy
- *is_contained_in*: $M \rightarrow F$ where *is_contained_in (m_i)=f_j* if the fact f_j contains the measure m_i
- *dimensions*: $D \rightarrow DI$ where *dimensions(d_i)=di_j* if the dimension d_i contributes to the dimensioning di_j
- *dimensioned_by*: $F \rightarrow DI$ where *dimensioned_by(f_i)=di_j* if the fact f_i is involved in the dimensioning di_j
- *is_part_of*: $SH \rightarrow H$ where *is_part_of(sh_i)=h_j* if sh_i is a sub-hierarchy of h_j
- *owner*: $A \rightarrow DL$ where *owner(a_i)=d_j* if a_i is an attribute of dimension level d_j
- *belongs_to*: $R \times H \rightarrow \tilde{N}$ where *belongs_to(r_i, h_j)=k* if the rollup r_i belongs to the hierarchy h_j and its order is equal to k
- *child*: $R \rightarrow DL$ where *child(r_i)=d_j* if the rollup r_i starts from dimension level d_j
- *parent*: $TR \rightarrow DL$ where *parent(tr_i)=d_j* if the target role tr_i goes to dimension level d_j
- *associated_to*: $R \times SH \rightarrow \tilde{N}$ where *associated_to(r_i, sh_j)=k* if the rollup r_i belongs to the subhierarchy sh_j and its order is equal to k
- *targets*: $R \rightarrow TR$ where *targets(r_i)=tr_j* if the rollup r_i has tr_j as target role
- *aggregates*: $M \rightarrow AF$ where *aggregates(m_i)=af_j* if the measure m_i may be aggregated using the function af_j
- *applicable*: $AF \rightarrow AT$ where *applicable(af_i)= at_j* if the aggregation function af_i corresponds to the aggregation type at_j i.e., the restriction level j

The main attributes correspond to mathematical functions between sets:

- *isIdentifyingAttribute*: $A \rightarrow \{true, false\}$ where *isIdentifyingAttribute(a_i)=true* if a_i identifies the dimension-level it describes and *isIdentifyingAttribute(a_i)=false* otherwise
- *isTime*: $DL \rightarrow \{true, false\}$ where *isTime(d_i)=true* if d_i is a temporal dimension level and *isTime(d_i)=false* if d_i is not a temporal dimension
- *restrictionlevel*: $AT \rightarrow \tilde{N}$ where *restrictionlevel(at_i)=i*
- *isStock*: $M \rightarrow \{true, false\}$ where *isStock(m_i)=true* if m_i is a stock measure and *isStock(m_i)=false* otherwise
- *isValuePerUnit*: $M \rightarrow \{true, false\}$ where *isValuePerUnit(m_i)=true* if m_i is a ratio and *isValuePerUnit(m_i)=false* otherwise
- *isElementary*: $M \rightarrow \{true, false\}$ where *isElementary(m_i)=true* if m_i is an elementary measure and *isElementary(m_i)=false* if m_i is a pre-aggregated measure
- *sourceLowerMultiplicity*: $R \times DL \rightarrow \{0,1\}$ where *sourceLowerMultiplicity(r_i, d_j)=0* if r_i is an incomplete drill-down and *1* otherwise
- *sourceUpperMultiplicity*: $R \times DL \rightarrow \{'1', '*'\}$ where *sourceUpperMultiplicity(r_i, d_j)='1'* if the corresponding drill-down is limited to one element or *'*'* otherwise
- *targetLowerMultiplicity*: $TR \rightarrow \{0,1\}$ where *targetLowerMultiplicity(tr_i)=0* if tr_i is a rollup incomplete hierarchy and *1* otherwise
- *targetUpperMultiplicity*: $TR \rightarrow \{'1', '*'\}$ where *targetUpperMultiplicity(tr_i)='*'* if the target tr_i is plural and *'1'* otherwise
- *targetCoeff*: $TR \rightarrow [0,1]$ where *targetCoeff(tr_i)* describes, in case of plural target, how the corresponding measure is shared between the different targets values
- *lowerMultiplicity*: $DI \rightarrow \{0,1\}$ where *lowerMultiplicity(di_i)=0* if di_i is a plural dimensioning and *1* otherwise
- *upperMultiplicity*: $DI \rightarrow \{'1', '*'\}$ where *upperMultiplicity(di_i)='*'* if the dimensioning di_i is plural and *'1'* otherwise
- *coeff*: $DI \rightarrow [0,1]$ where *coeff(di_i)* describes, in case of plural dimensioning, how the corresponding measure is shared between the different dimension levels
- *summarizabilityAlongHierarchy*: $H \times M \rightarrow AT$ where *summarizabilityAlongHierarchy(h_i, m_j)=at_k* if all aggregations of measure m_j along hierarchy h_i are of type at_k. In the same way, we define the function *summarizabilityAlongSubHierarchy* and the function *summarizabilityAlongDimension*.

This formal specification increases the expressiveness of the meta-model and facilitates the automation of the transformation rules presented below.

4.2 Transformation Rules

Mapping rules **R1** to **R12** transform source meta-model main classes (fact, dimension level, measure, attribute, dimension, hierarchy, subhierarchy, aggregation function, aggregation type, target role, rollup, dimensioning) into nodes, thus allowing them to be directly connected to each other and to any other component of the database. It also allows different measures to be easily connected to a common fact and a given fact to be linked to its dimension levels. Finally, the dimension levels may be connected through different rollups inside hierarchies. These choices, at the logical level, allow us to ensure that the richness of the concepts of the source model is preserved. Rules **R13** to **R16** transform the four main UML aggregations into corresponding edges labelled respectively: IS_*CONTAINED_IN, OWNER, COMPOSED_OF,* and: *IS_PART_OF*. Rules **R17** to **R19** transform the three main UML compositions into corresponding edges labelled respectively: BELONGS_*TO, ASSOCIATED_TO,* and: *APPLICABLE*. Rules **R20** to **R22** transform the three UML main associations into corresponding edges labelled: AGGREGATES, *IS_DIVIDED_ALONG,* and: *IS_DISPATCHED _ALONG*. Rules **R23** to **R27** transform the three main UML association classes *Dimensioning, SourceRole* and *TargetRole* into the corresponding edges. Finally, rules **R28** to **R30** transfer the information on applicable aggregation functions from conceptual multidimensional to logical graph model to be actionable at the physical level.

R1: Each fact $f_i \in F$ is mapped to a node $no \in NO$ where $no.label=:Fact$ and $no.type=f_i$

R2, R3, R4, R5, R6, R7, R8, R11, and **R12** similarly map respectively dimension levels, dimensions, measures, attributes, rollups, hierarchies, subhierarchies, aggregation functions, and aggregation types to respective labelled nodes.

R9: Each target role $tr_i \in TR$ is mapped to a node $no \in NO$ where $no.label=:TargetRole$ and $no.type=tr_i$ and $no.isPlural=isPlural(tr_i)$ and $no.targetLowerMultiplicity=targetLowerMultiplicity(tr_i)$ and $no.tartgetUpperMultiplicity=targetUpperMultiplicity(tr_i)$ and $no.targetCoeff=targetCoeff(tr_i)$

R10: Each dimensioning $di_i \in DI$ is mapped to a node $no \in NO$ where $no.label=:Dimensioning$ and $no.type=di_i$ and $no.lowerMultiplicity=lowerMultiplicity(di_i)$ and $no.upperMultiplicity=upperMultiplicity(di_i)$ and $no.coeff=coeff(di_i)$

R13: Each composition relationship between a measure $m_i \in M$ and a fact $f_i \in F$ is mapped to an edge $e \in ED$ where $e.label=:IS\_CONTAINED\_IN$ and $e.tail=no_1$ and $e.head=no_2$ where no_1 and no_2 are the nodes representing m_i and f_j.

R14, R15, R16, R17, R18, R19, R20, R21, R22, R23, R24, R25 and **R27** similarly map ownership (between attribute and dimension level), composition between hierarchy and dimension, composition between subhierarchy and hierarchy, membership link between rollup and hierarchy, membership link between rollup and subhierarchy, relationship between aggregation function and type, relationship between measure and aggregation function, relationship between target role and measure, relationship between plural dimensioning and measure, link between dimension and dimensioning, link between fact and dimensioning, parent link between target role and dimension level, link between rollup and target role, to respective edges labelled :OWNER, :COMPOSED_OF, :IS_PART_OF, :BELONGS_TO, :ASSOCIATED_TO, :APPLICABLE,:AGGREGATES, :IS_DIVIDED_ALONG,:IS_DISPATCHED_ALONG, :DIMENSIONS, :DIMENSIONED_BY, :PARENT, :TARGETS.

R26: Each child link between a rollup $r_i \in R$ and a dimension level $dl_j \in DL$ is mapped to an edge $e \in ED$ where $e.label=:CHILD$ and $e.tail=no_1$ and $e.head=no_2$ where no_1 and no_2 are the nodes representing r_i and dl_j and $e.lowerMultiplicity=sourceLowerMultiplicity(r_i,dl_j)$ and $e.upperMultiplicity=sourceUpperMultiplicity(r_i,dl_j)$

R28: Each SummarizabilityAlongHierarchy association between a measure $m_i \in M$, a hierarchy $h_j \in H$ and an aggregation type at_k is mapped to a node $no \in NO$ where $no.label=:SummarizabilityAlongHierarchy$ and $no.type= m_i|h_j$ (concatenation of m_i and h_j) and to three edges $e_1 \in ED$, $e_2 \in ED$ and $e_3 \in ED$ where $e_1.label =:ALONG$ and $e_1.tail=no$ and $e_1.head=no_1$ and $e_2.label=:FOR\_MEASURE$ and $e_2.tail=no$ and $e_2.head=no_2$ and $e_3.label=:AGGREGATING$ and $e_3.tail=no$ and $e_3.head=no_3$ where no_1, no_2 and no_3 are nodes representing h_j, m_i and at_k

R29 and **R30** similarly map SummarizabilityAlongSubHierarchy association between measure and subhierarchy and SummarizabilityAlongDimension association between measure and dimension to respective edges also labeled :ALONG, :FOR_MEASURE, and :AGGREGATING.

The result of the transformation is a logical schema. Transforming the latter to a physical schema involves adding instances and, if required by frequent queries, optimizing the resulting graph. This physical step is beyond the scope of this paper.

4.3 Application of the Approach to the Motivating Example

The application of the rules allows us to obtain a logical graph (Fig. 3). The mapping strategy intends to take maximum advantage of the representational power of directed labeled edges and the expressiveness of languages based on the traversal of such paths.

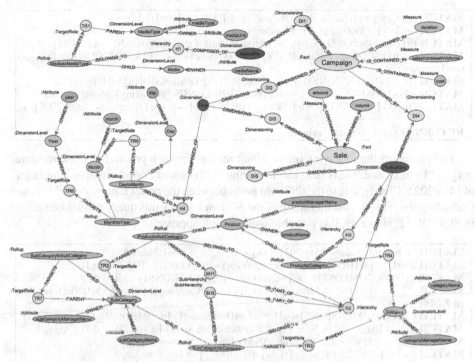

Fig. 3. Resulting graph (partial representation)

5 Validation of the Approach

At the logical level, mapping validation can be performed using schema-based approaches, i.e. by reasoning on the mapped schemas and the mapping definition [14]. We base our validation on checking three desirable properties, i.e. satisfiability, inference, and losslessness, proposed in [17]. For space reasons, only the losslessness is described.

Mapping losslessness property requires to provide a query on the source schema (in our case a multidimensional schema), and to check whether all the data needed to answer that query is mapped into the target schema (i.e. graph schema). To this effect, we derived, from the syntax of the query language Cypher, a syntax to formulate multidimensional queries on our graph structure. For space reasons, we do not provide the corresponding grammar. We illustrate it with two queries.

Assume the following query: return the total amount of cars purchased each year. The SQL query is defined below:

```
SELECT ye.year, sum(sa.amount) FROM Sale sa, Product pr, Category ca, Day da,
Month mo, Year ye WHERE sa.productName=pr.productName AND sa.day=da.day
AND da.month=mo.month AND mo.year=ye.year AND ca.categoryName='car'
GROUP BY ye.year;
```

The corresponding graph query adapted from Cypher for Neo4j is defined below:

```
MATCH (ct :Category{categoryName= "car"})<-[:PARENT]- (tr1:TR4)
MATCH (tr1) <- [:TARGETS] - (pcl:ProducttoCategory) - [:BELONGS_TO] -> (h1:H3)
MATCH (h1) -[:COMPOSED_OF] - (pd1:ProductDim) -[ :DIMENSIONS] -> (di1:DI5)
MATCH    (di1)<-[:DIMENSIONED_BY]  -  (s1:Sale)  <-  [:IS_CONTAINED_IN]  -
(am1:amount)
MATCH (s1) - [:DIMENSIONED_BY] -> (di2:DI3) <-[:DIMENSIONS] - (t1:Time)
MATCH (t1) - [COMPOSED_OF] -> (h2:H4) <- [:BELONGS_TO] - (my1:MonthtoYear)
MATCH (my1)-[:TARGETS]->(tr1:TR6) - [:PARENT] -> (ye1:Year) <- [:OWNER] -
(y1:year)
RETURN y1.value, sum(am1.value)
```

Let's consider the following query which returns for each product of the same category as "Renault Zoé" the benefit earned during the "Renault Zoé advertising campaign"
of May 2021. Clearly, due to the different paths between the nodes *Category* and *Product*
(including the cycle for the hierarchy of the *Subcategories*), this query cannot be written
in SQL OLAP. However, it is possible with a graph approach.

```
MATCH (m1:month{value="May 2021"}) - [:OWNER] -> (mo1:Month)
MATCH (mo1) <- [:CHILD] - (my1: MonthtoYear) - [:BELONGS_TO] -> (h1: H4)
MATCH (h1) <- [:COMPOSED_OF] - (t1:Time) - [:DIMENSIONS] -> (di1:DI2)
MATCH          (di1)<-[:DIMENSIONED_BY]-(ca1:Campaign)-[:DIMENSIONED_BY]->
(di2:DI4)
MATCH (di2) <- [DIMENSIONS] -(pd1:ProductDimension) - [:COMPOSED_OF] -> (h2:H3)
MATCH (h2) <- [:BELONGS_TO] -  (pc1:ProducttoCategory) - [:CHILD] -> (pr1:Product)
MATCH (pr1) <- [:OWNER] - (p1:productName{value="Renault Zoé"})
MATCH (pc1) - [:TARGETS] -> (tr1:TR4) -[:PARENT] -> (ct1:Category)
MATCH (ct1) -- (pr2:Product) <- [:OWNER] - (p2:productName)
MATCH (pr2) -- (s1:Sale) <- [:IS_CONTAINED_IN] - (a1:amount)
MATCH (s1) <- [:IS_CONTAINED_IN] - (v1:volume)
RETURN p2.value, sum(a1.value*v1.value)
```

Observe that the *MATCH (ct1) -- (pr2:Product)* step allows to consider all existing
paths between the node *Category* and *Product*.

As a conclusion, we were able to translate classical OLAP queries as well as more
complex queries exploiting the richness of our source multidimensional model (i.e.
mainly plural dimensionings and rollups on non-strict and reflexive hierarchies). These
are promising results even if we need more experiments to evaluate the performance.

6   Conclusion and Future Research

This paper has mostly proposed a logical mapping of a multidimensional data warehouse
meta-model to a NoSQL graph meta-model. A comprehensive set of transformation
rules have been proposed. We have illustrated these mapping rules on a case study. We
have enriched Cypher language to enable multidimensional queries on graphs. We have
proposed a validation process to verify the losslessness property. A main advantage is
that we consider, at a conceptual level, all the specific cases of hierarchies (multiple,
non-strict, reflexive) and complex problems of fact dimensioning.

Several questions remain open. The mapping transformations need to be enriched to
also include the physical level with instances. We have to experiment the approach on
extensive case studies. Evaluating the performance of the target model will be required

to validate the whole approach, from conceptual to physical levels. The choice of the target graph-processing engine will be crucial. One possibility is to test EmptyHeaded that seems to allow both a high-level query language and good response time [1].

References

1. Aberger, C.R., Lamb, A., Tu, S., Nötzli, A., Olukotun, K., Ré, C.: EmptyHeaded: a relational engine for graph processing. Trans. Database Syst. **42**(4), 1–44 (2017)
2. Beheshti, S.-M.-R., Benatallah, B., Motahari-Nezhad, H.R.: Scalable graph-based OLAP analytics over process execution data. Distrib. Parallel Databases **34**(3), 379–423 (2014). https://doi.org/10.1007/s10619-014-7171-9
3. Besta, M., et al.: Demystifying graph databases: analysis and taxonomy of data organization, system designs, and graph queries. arXiv preprint arXiv:1910.09017 (2019)
4. Blaschka, M., Sapia, C., Höfling, G.: On schema evolution in multidimensional databases. In: Mohania, M., Tjoa, A.M. (eds.) DaWaK 1999. LNCS, vol. 1676, pp. 153–164. Springer, Heidelberg (1999). https://doi.org/10.1007/3-540-48298-9_17
5. Boussahoua, M., Boussaid, O., Bentayeb, F.: Logical schema for data warehouse on column-oriented NoSQL databases. In: Benslimane, D., Damiani, E., Grosky, W.I., Hameurlain, A., Sheth, A., Wagner, R.R. (eds.) DEXA 2017. LNCS, vol. 10439, pp. 247–256. Springer, Cham (2017). https://doi.org/10.1007/978-3-319-64471-4_20
6. Castelltort, A., Laurent, A.: NoSQL graph-based OLAP analysis. In: Proceedings of KDIR (2014)
7. Chevalier, M., El Malki, M., Kopliku, A., Teste, O., Tournier, R.: Implementation of multi-dimensional databases in column-oriented NoSQL systems. In: Tadeusz, M., Valduriez, P., Bellatreche, L. (eds.) Advances in Databases and Information Systems. ADBIS 2015. Lecture Notes in Computer Science, vol. 9282, pp. 79–91, Springer, Cham (2015). https://doi.org/10.1007/978-3-319-23135-8_6
8. Chevalier, M., El Malki, M., Kopliku, A., Teste, O., Tournier, R.: Implementation of multidimensional databases with document-oriented NoSQL. In: Madria, S., Hara, T. (eds.) Big Data Analytics and Knowledge Discovery. DaWaK 2015. Lecture Notes in Computer Science, vol. 9263, pp. 379–390. Springer, Cham (2015). https://doi.org/10.1007/978-3-319-22729-0_29
9. Chouder, M.L., Rizzi, S., Chalal, R.: Exodus: exploratory OLAP over document stores. Inform. Syst. **79**, 44–57 (2019)
10. Daniel, G., Sunyé, G., Cabot, J.: UMLtoGraphDB: mapping conceptual schemas to graph databases. In: Comyn-Wattiau, I., Tanaka, K., Song, I.-Y., Yamamoto, S., Saeki, M. (eds.) ER 2016. LNCS, vol. 9974, pp. 430–444. Springer, Cham (2016). https://doi.org/10.1007/978-3-319-46397-1_33
11. Dehdouh, K.: Building OLAP cubes from columnar NoSQL data warehouses. In: Bellatreche, L., Pastor, Ó., Almendros, J.J., Aït-Ameur, Y. (eds.) Model and Data Engineering MEDI 2016. Lecture Notes in Computer Science, vol. 9893, pp. 166–179. Springer, Cham (2016). https://doi.org/10.1007/978-3-319-45547-1_14
12. Fan, J., Raj, A.G.S., Patel, J.M.: The case against specialized graph analytics engines. In 7th Biennial Conference on Innovative Data Systems Research (CIDR 2015), USA (2015)
13. Lissandrini, M., Brugnara, M., Velegrakis, Y.: Beyond macrobenchmarks: microbenchmark-based graph database evaluation. Proc. VLDB Endow. **12**(4), 390–403 (2018)
14. Madhavan, J., Bernstein, P.A., Domingos, P., Halevy, A.Y.: Representing and reasoning about mappings between domain models. In: Proceedings of AAAI/IAAI (2002)
15. Naydenova, I., Kaloyanova, K.: Sparsity handling and data explosion in OLAP systems. MCIS **10**, 62–70 (2010)

16. Prat, N., Akoka, J., Comyn-Wattiau, I.: A UML-based data warehouse design method. Decis. Support Syst. **42**(3), 1449–1473 (2006)
17. Rull Fort, G.: Validation of mappings between data schemas. Universitat Politècnica de Catalunya, Ph.D. thesis (2011)
18. Sellami, A., Nabli, A., Gargouri, F.: Transformation of data warehouse schema to NoSQL graph data base. In: Abraham, A., Cherukuri, A.K., Melin, P., Gandhi, N. (eds.) ISDA 2018 2018. AISC, vol. 941, pp. 410–420. Springer, Cham (2020). https://doi.org/10.1007/978-3-030-16660-1_41
19. Vyawahare, H.R., Karde, P.P., Thakare, V.M.: A hybrid database approach using graph and relational database. In: IEEE International RICE Conference, pp. 1–4 (2018)
20. Yangui, R., Nabli, A., Gargouri, F.: Automatic transformation of data warehouse schema to NoSQL data base: comparative study. In: Proceedings of KES, pp. 255–264 (2016)

Designing Document Databases:
A Comprehensive Requirements Perspective

Noa Roy-Hubara[1]([✉]), Arnon Sturm[1], and Peretz Shoval[1,2]

[1] Ben-Gurion University of the Negev, Beer Sheva, Israel
nro@post.bgu.ac.il, {sturm,shoval}@bgu.ac.il
[2] Netanya Academic College, Netanya, Israel

Abstract. The new data characteristics led to the development of new databases models and systems, namely NoSQL. Among these, document databases gain a lot of attention. While their usage is fast-growing, design methods for such databases received little attention. In this paper, we present a new method for designing document databases. The proposed method is based on a conceptual model of the application domain and considers the data-related functional requirements. We propose a set of rules to be applied to transform the conceptual model of the application, and its functional requirements, into a document database schema.

Keywords: NoSQL · Conceptual modeling · Document database · Database design

1 Introduction

The new digital era has brought about the rise of new database types, most notably NoSQL databases, which comprise four sub-types: document databases, column-based databases, key-value databases, and graph databases. While designing relational databases has been treated intensively for many years, the design of NoSQL databases is in its incubation phase and requires further attention. In a literature review, we found that new design methods for these databases are still in their development stage [8].

In this paper, we focus on the design of document databases. Such databases gain a lot of attention. The leading vendor of such databases, MongoDB, closely follows the usage of relational databases[1]. As of this growth, we aim at addressing the design of such a database. As their name implies, document databases consist of collections of documents. A document is a set of name-value pairs, usually in JSON format. Those pairs represent the document's properties. Unlike SQL, documents (equivalent to records in the relational model terminology) in a collection (equivalent to table) may vary in their properties.

Some document design methods propose new and innovative concepts or insights, but they lack inclusiveness or formality. This paper further examines and uses some concepts and proposes a structured design process. Following our previous work on

---

[1] https://db-engines.com/en/ranking.

© Springer Nature Switzerland AG 2021
I. Reinhartz-Berger and S. Sadiq (Eds.): ER 2021 Workshops, LNCS 13012, pp. 15–25, 2021.
https://doi.org/10.1007/978-3-030-88358-4_2

selecting database models [7], we propose a method that follows model-based principles that can later be unified.

The rest of this paper is structured as follows: In Sect. 2 we set the background for designing document databases. In Sect. 3 we refer to the existing methods and analyze their shortcomings. In Sect. 4 we introduce the proposed design method, and in Sect. 5 we conclude and set plans for future research.

2 Basics of Document Databases

To set the ground for designing document databases, we start by introducing the structure of document databases. A document database consists of the following:

- **Document Collection.** A **Document** represents an entity in the real world. A **Document collection** consists of documents of the same "type". A document has a name and potential properties. One of the properties is a key, which facilitates unique identification.
- **Property.** As said, a document in a collection has properties. Properties may vary between documents in the same collection. A property may be of a complex type.
- **Embedded Relationship.** In a document database, there may be a "document within a document" – embedding connected data in a single document.
- **Referenced Relationship.** A referenced relationship requires a key of one document to be referenced inside another document.

The implications of such a database structure are the following:

- Documents of the same collection may vary in properties (e.g., one document representing a person may possess a "children" property, while other documents may not). However, it is important to try and define all **possible** properties of a document in a collection to avoid inconsistencies.
- The decision on a relationship type (reference vs. embedded) is important and is one of the main questions which requires examination when modeling a document database.
- NoSQL in general, and document databases in particular, do not adhere to the concepts of data-redundancy that exist in relational databases. Therefore, data may be duplicated in a document database. Duplication could exist if it contributes to the modeling and performance and does not contradict other database requirements.

3 Related Work

The area of designing document databases has gained some attention. However, it is still in its incubation phase, as there is no single mature, popular, and inclusive method. In this section, we review some of the proposed methods and analyze their strengths and weaknesses. Indeed, some of those methods introduce essential concepts, experiments or notions, and thus we adopt them to propose a comprehensive method.

The first design method that references document databases is NoAM [2], which is an inclusive method for designing NoSQL databases, excluding graph databases. The method is based on new concepts such as blocks and aggregates, which are based on a conceptual model and access patterns. The authors implemented a use case on three data models, one of which is the document data model and MongoDB. Since the method is very inclusive, it is also rather complicated and requires learning new concepts. It also lacks formality. The authors performed a simple evaluation of different possibilities of the data representation suggested by the NoAM method in Oracle NoSQL.

Varga et al. [10] propose a method that uses formal concept analysis (FCA), or rather Relational Concept Analysis (RCA), which extends FCA as a data model. According to the authors, "The objective of RCA is to build a set of lattices whose concepts are related by relational attributes, similar to UML associations". The method uses Entity-Relationship (ER) as a conceptual model, that is transformed into a Relational Context Family, which is the structure of data within the RCA. The method references the two different relationship types in document databases, which is very important in document modeling. Furthermore, it considers the cardinality between entities to choose the proper kind of relationship. When the two relationship types are possible based on cardinality, they do not suggest other means of distinction.

De Lima and Dos Santos Mello [3] suggest a method based on EER and queries workloads. The workload information is estimated over the conceptual schema, i.e., the size of each construct in the EER. This is used to estimate the number of accesses for each construct based on access patterns, which in turn is applied in choosing between the different relationship types. The method introduces essential concepts such as the use of the workloads. The rules and functions themselves are based on cardinality, but this concept is not explained.

Imam et al. [6] suggest new cardinality concepts in which the "many" cardinality is broken down into several levels – few, many, and squillions. While the paper mainly suggests new styles for the conceptual model, it also demonstrates important experiments that assist in choosing the right kind of relationship in the final database.

Similarly, Herrero et al. [4] present a method for designing NoSQL databases based on traditional design approaches. The method consists of seven steps, spanning over the three phases of the conventional design (conceptual, logical, and physical). We particularly noticed the fourth step as it sheds light on the design of the relationship types. This method is more general and mainly addresses analytical workloads.

Other methods that we have reviewed include (1) an inclusive method suggested by Banerjee et al. [1] that uses GOOSSDM (Graph Object-Oriented Semi-Structured Data Model) as a conceptual model; (2) a simple method by Shin et al. [9] that transforms an ER diagram into a document logical model without other considerations; and (3) an algorithm by Imam et al. [5] that considers the application's entities, their expected number of records, CRUD operations and other NFRs (Availability, Consistency, Security) for creating a document schema.

To summarize, several studies propose methods for document database design. However, it seems that while each study introduces important concepts, a more inclusive design method is still needed, one that takes into account all types of requirements, that uses formal concepts, and that is also easy to learn and use.

4   The Requirement-Based Document Database Design Method

In this section, we introduce the Requirement-based Document Database Design (RbDDD) method. We begin with presenting an example of an application and its requirements, followed by the proposed rules and guidelines of transforming the requirements into a document database schema. The result is at a **logical level,** independent of physical aspects and a specific database provider.

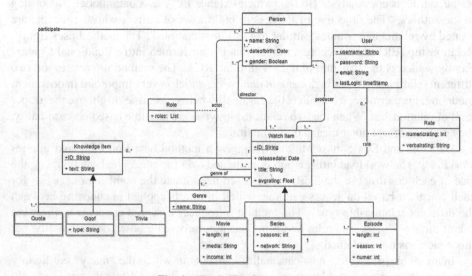

Fig. 1. The IMDb Class diagram

-    **Query 1**. Simple search (RETURN ALL FROM WatchItem WHERE title = ?)
-    **Query 2**. Find person by role (RETURN ALL FROM WatchItem, Person WHERE rel.role like ?)
-    **Query 3**. Recommendation query (RETURN rec.title FROM watchItem as rec, watchItem AS org WHERE org.Genre = rec.Genre and type(org)=type(rec) and rec.releasedate BETWEEN org.releasedate += 10)
-    **Query 4**. ALL persons (of type) for a watch item (RETURN Person.All FROM Watch Item, Person WHERE title = ? and rel = Actor)

Listing 1. A List of the IMDb System queries

4.1   The IMDb Example

The IMDB system stores data about movies, series, and episodes (for all of which we use the term "watch-item") and provides search and recommendation services for its users. The requirements for RbDDD are expressed as: a) the data requirements are expressed as a Class diagram, as presented in Fig. 1; and b) the functional requirements are expressed as queries, as presented in Listing 1, using an SQL-like syntax. This syntax is easy to use as it is very similar to SQL, but without complex issues such as Joins [7]. Relevant queries are of retrieval and update [7], and any formal query language can be used for that purpose.

4.2 Transformation Rules

When discussing the design of a document database, we need to refer to the way relationships are represented, as it is a most crucial modeling aspect in the document database and highly affects performance. With that in mind, two aspects need to be considered.

- **Multi-Embedding** describes a document that is embedded in several documents and possibly in different contexts. For example, a "Person" entity with ID "A" may be embedded in a "Movie" entity as a producer, in another "Movie" entity as a director, and in a "Quote" entity as a participant. If such cases are possible, we should examine if an embedded entity is the best modeling option, since an update of this entity will require many accesses to the database and may result in short-term consistency issues. Since currently we mainly address manipulation queries, we allow multi-embedding.
- **Absolute vs. Partial Embedding.** Absolute embedding means that the embedded entity will not be addressed independently and will only exist as an embedded entity. Partial embedding means that the embedded entity requires existence outside of the embedded scope and exists as an independent entity. Currently, our method will apply only absolute embedding, as partial embedding requires further analysis if and when it is required vs. the impact on the database size and consistency. We plan to address this issue in future work.

We demonstrate how different types of relationships in the conceptual model are transformed into the document database relationship types.

Hierarchy (Inheritance/is-a Relationship)

Handling hierarchy should consider two issues: *hierarchy constraints* (Complete and Disjoint/Overlap in UML class diagram), and *queries* that involve the classes in the hierarchy. In addressing these considerations, three alternatives exist:

The first alternative is to create one class representing all classes in the relationships – the super-class. It means, removing the sub-classes and moving their attributes and relationships up to the super-class. If a distinction between the different sub-classes is required, a new property named "type" can be added, although the type can be implicitly inferred based on the attributes that exist in the instances of each class.

The second alternative is to define a class for each sub-class only. It means, removing the super-class and moving its properties and relationships to each of its sub-classes.

The third alternative is creating a class for each class in the hierarchy – the super-class and the sub-classes. This requires adding a new relationship "hierarchy" between the super-class and its sub-classes. Such design will require at least two reads when information regarding a sub-class is required: one for the properties of the super-class and one for the properties of the sub-classes related to it with the "hierarchy" relationship. An elementary recommendation by MongoDB[2] is to structure the schema so that the application will receive all the required information in **one read**. Since implementing this alternative will increase the number of reads, we currently do not consider it.

---

[2] https://docs.mongodb.com/manual/tutorial/model-embedded-one-to-many-relationships-bet ween-documents/.

The conversion rules for hierarchies are as follows:

Rule 1

1. In case that at most one hierarchy constraint is defined, remove the sub-classes. We chose this strategy because there are objects in the super-class that are not one any of the sub-classes, or that an object of a class may belong to many sub-classes.
2. In case that both Complete and Disjoint constraints are defined on the hierarchy, the relevant queries should be examined.

   a. If a query that references the super-class and no other classes in the "from" part of the query exists (i.e., no relationship is required in the query), we choose to remove the sub-classes, as in the case 1.
   b. If no such query exists, we choose to remove the super-class. This mapping is chosen since all objects of the super-class belong to one sub-class only, and there is no direct query that requires the super-class. Therefore, there is no need to maintain the super-class.

In our example, we have an inheritance hierarchy where Episode, Movie, and Series are sub-classes of WatchItem. Since no other types of watch item exist, and the constraint is disjoint, we need to check if there is a query that references the super-class and no other class in the "from" part of the query exists. Listing 1 indicates that such a query exists (#1). It requires a search based on a title and returns any watch item with that title, as in the real IMDb[3].

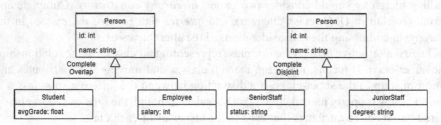

Fig. 2. Hierarchy examples

Figure 2 shows another example: On the left side, a hierarchy relation is defined with Complete and Overlap constraints: a person may be both an employee and a student, but no other types of Person exist. Therefore, in the conversion process, we use part 1 of rule 1, and the database will include only classes of the super-class with all possible properties in the sub-classes. On the right side of the figure, the hierarchy relation is defined with Complete and Disjoint constraints: a person must be either SeniorStaff **or** JuniorStaff. In this case, we review the queries that use this relation: if a query in which "Person" is queried in the "from" part of the query with no other class exist, then we

---

[3] https://www.imdb.com/find?s=tt&q=A+HARD+DAY%27S+NIGHT&ref_=nv_sr_sm.

use the same mapping as in the previous example; otherwise, we remove the super-class and move its properties to the sub-classes.

Aggregation and Composition

Aggregation relationship in a UML class diagram is a binary association between a composite class and its dependent classes. In such relationship, an object in the the the dependent classes may exist if the relationships are eliminated. **Composition**, on the other hand, is a stronger type of aggregation in which an object in the dependent class must be associated with at most one composite class.

We can address both types of relationships based on their cardinality: if not stated otherwise in the class diagram, aggregation as many-to-many relationship, and composition as one-to-many relationships. Therefore, we convert both types of relationships to "regular" relationships and complete the conversion based on their cardinalities.

Cardinality Constraints

We distinguish between one-to-one, one-to-many, and many-to-many constraints:

One-to-One

According to Imam et al. [6], based on performed experiments, the authors concluded that one-to-one relationships have better performance when created as embedded. However, that paper did not discuss how and if such embedding is possible. A description for such cases may be found in the concept lattices in Varga et al. [10]. These lattices describe possible embeddings based on the *minimum* part of the constraint: $(0, 1) \rightarrow (0, 1)$, $(0, 1) \rightarrow (1, 1)$, $(1, 1) \rightarrow (0, 1)$, and $(1, 1) \rightarrow (1, 1)$. We will split our explanation into two possible cases. Since such a relationship does not exist in our movies example, we will demonstrate it with different examples.

In case that the minimum constraint of a class is 0, we are unable to embed another class within it; such embedding would result in data loss. Examples are shown in Fig. 3: a person **may** have a passport, but not more than one; a passport belongs to one person only. If we choose to embed the Person class within the Passport class, all persons who have no passport will be lost. Such cases require partial embedding, but we currently do not discuss this matter.

In case that the minimum constraint is 1, embedding is possible. In relationships such as the third example in Fig. 3, we must choose the best possible embedding between the two possible options; we choose the embedding based on the **read** queries. In the said case of one-to-one relationships with $(1, 1)$ constraint, we choose to embed the **less** queried class into the more **frequently** queried class, so to be able to get all information in one read. In the example, we assume that we need to read more frequently the Person class (room details, payment details, ticket details, etc.), as opposed to ticket details. This leads to embed the ticket class within the person class.

Based on the above we define the following rule:

Rule 2

In One-to-One relationships, we consider the minimum cardinality constraint:

a. If for both classes the minimum is 0, then embedding is impossible, and a two-way reference relationship should be created.

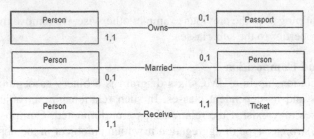

Fig. 3. One-to-One example

b. If one of the classes has a minimum 0, and the other has a minimum 1, then we embed the "may be" class (0) within the mandatory class (1)
c. If both classes have a minimum 1, embedding is possible in both directions. In such cases we embed the less read-queried class into the more read-queried class.

One-to-Many
In the case of one-to-many constraint, Imam et al. differentiate between three types of "many": Few (7 documents, denoted as F), Many (5,000 denoted as M) and Squillion (500,000 denoted as S) [6]. We currently focus on Many and Few types, since Squillion may appear in rare cases. In their experiments, 1-to-F relationships performed better when embedding, while 1-to-M relationships performed better when referencing. In their experiments the authors distinguished between reading and writing; and it seems that in reading the difference was rather small and not clear if statistically significant.

Due to these experiments and the MongoDB recommendation, as discussed previously, in which we should reduce the number of operations for obtaining needed data, we recommend embedding one-to-many relationships as well. As in the case of one-to-one relationships, embedding is only possible when the minimum for embedded side is 1 - not 0. Herrero et al. suggest in such relationships to embed the 1-side of the relationship into the many-side of the relationship [4]. This is probably due to possible data duplication and what we defined as multi-embedding. However, in NoSQL data duplication is not a major issue as in RDBMS, and sometimes it is required to achieve the needed data with minimum reads. Therefore, we claim that embedding is possible in both directions in such relationships, and that it highly depends on the read queries.

In Fig. 4 we zoom-in on two scenarios of one-to-many relationships, taken from the class diagram in Fig. 1. The first relationship is between Knowledge-Item and its Watch-Item, and the second is between Series and its Episodes. In both cases we prefer to embed the "many" into the "one", as opposed to what is suggested by Herrero et al. [4], due to the possible queries. E.g., we will probably have Select queries regarding a Watch-item (and its related knowledge items, aka quotes, trivia-items, etc.), and less individual queries on a Knowledge item (i.e., a knowledge item **of a watch item** as opposed to knowledge item without its related watch item). This is also the case with Series and its Episodes. The reverse embedding of "one" in the "many" class is of course possible, as will be shown in the formal rule.

Based on the above, we define the following rule:

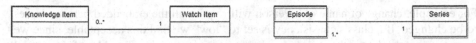

Fig. 4. One-to-Many examples

Rule 3

1. We observe the "read" functional requirements regarding the classes in the relationship. we use several counters:

    i.   how many times each class appear as the subject of "read" queries, generally;
    ii. how many "read" queries are required for both classes together; and
    iii. how many times they are the subject of "read" queries **when queried together**.

    For example, in the query "for a Lecturer, return all its classes" the subject is Lecturer, while in the query "return all information for a Class, including its lecturer" the subject is "Class"

2. If "read" queries of both classes together exist (i.e., counter #2 > 0) then embedding is based on the third counter, and we embed the class with the smaller counter into the class with the larger counter, if possible (i.e., if minimum cardinality is 1).

3. Else, embed based on the first counter: embed the class with the smaller counter into the class with the larger counter, if possible (i.e., minimum cardinality is 1).

4. If embedding was not performed, create a two-way reference relationship.

Many-to-Many

Most current methods and reviews do not suggest embedding documents in many-to-many relationships. One such example is by Imam et al. who performed several experiments with different cardinalities and sizes [6]. The results clearly showed that both writing time and reading time largely reduces in reference type relationships with cardinality of many-to-many. Due to these results, we do not consider embedding such relationships, and thus create two-way reference relationship.

Manual Changes

Our design rules may be subject to manual changes, possibly depending on system requirements, most notably the requirements of Consistency and Flexibility. In Consistency, we refer to the notion that data in database is always valid (Strong consistency) or Eventually consistent. In flexibility we refer to database changes that might be required.

For example, Herrero et al. state that one-to-many relationships will be merged (to-one merged within the to-many) if the to-one end represents a Slowly-Changing-Dimension (SCD) – a notion from the DW world that identifies relatively static data. Relatively static data [4] (in our notations: data with low flexibility [7]) do not require many changes and therefore its updates are minimal, even if the to-one class is embedded in many classes (in our notations: multi-embedding). However, since document database are more "read" optimized, we do not address the issue of many writes.

Another issue regards consistency: if a class is embedded within several other classes and requires updates, it is possible that the database will not be consistent for some time.

For example, change of name of a Person will require all the embedded person classes to be changed. If a class's consistency is set to "low" we find this acceptable, since we do not expect the data in the class to be always consistent, and we would prefer to model the data for best performance. However, if consistency is set to "high", we need to look further into our model.

5 Summary and Future Work

We introduced a method for designing document databases based on data requirements expressed as a Class diagram and functional requirements expressed as data-related queries. The method transforms the relationships in the class diagram into document-database embedded and referenced relationships. We introduced rules for the said transformation. A preliminary evaluation that we performed on the IMDb example indicated an improvement over a reference-based solution.

Future work includes strengthening the rules, adding association classes, and implementing the transformation rules in a software tool. In addition, we plan to add workload information to the queries and adjust the rules accordingly. Finally, we plan to evaluate method in real-world case studies on a document-database platform.

References

1. Banerjee, S., Shaw, R., Sarkar, A., Debnath, N.C.: Towards logical level design of big data. In: 2015 IEEE 13th International Conference on Industrial Informatics (INDIN), pp. 1665–1671. IEEE, July 2015
2. Bugiotti, F., Cabibbo, L., Atzeni, P., Torlone, R.: Database design for NoSQL systems. In: Yu, E., Dobbie, G., Jarke, M., Purao, S. (eds.) ER 2014. LNCS, vol. 8824, pp. 223–231. Springer, Cham (2014). https://doi.org/10.1007/978-3-319-12206-9_18
3. de Lima, C., dos Santos Mello, R.: A workload-driven logical design approach for NoSQL document databases. In: Proceedings of the 17th International Conference on Information Integration and Web-based Applications & Services, pp. 1–10, December 2015
4. Herrero, V., Abelló, A., Romero, O.: NOSQL design for analytical workloads: variability matters. In: Comyn-Wattiau, I., Tanaka, K., Song, I.Y., Yamamoto, S., Saeki, M. (eds.) ER 2016. LNCS, vol. 9974, pp. 50–64. Springer, Cham (2016). https://doi.org/10.1007/978-3-319-46397-1_4
5. Imam, A.A., Basri, S., Ahmad, R., Watada, J., González-Aparicio, M.T.: Automatic schema suggestion model for NoSQL document-stores databases. J. Big Data 5(1), 1–17 (2018). https://doi.org/10.1186/s40537-018-0156-1
6. Imam, A.A., Basri, S., Ahmad, R., Aziz, N., González-Aparicio, M.T.: New cardinality notations and styles for modeling NoSQL document-store databases. In: TENCON 2017–2017 IEEE Region 10 Conference, pp. 2765–2770. IEEE, November 2017
7. Roy-Hubara, N., Shoval, P., Sturm, A.: A method for database model selection. In: Reinhartz-Berger, I., Zdravkovic, J., Gulden, J., Schmidt, R. (eds.) BPMDS/EMMSAD -2019. LNBIP, vol. 352, pp. 261–275. Springer, Cham (2019). https://doi.org/10.1007/978-3-030-20618-5_18
8. Roy-Hubara, N., Sturm, A.: Design methods for the new database era: a systematic literature review. Softw. Syst. Model. 19(2), 297–312 (2019). https://doi.org/10.1007/s10270-019-00739-8

9. Shin, K., Hwang, C., Jung, H.: NoSQL database design using UML conceptual data model based on Peter Chen's framework. Int. J. Appl. Eng. Res. **12**(5), 632–636 (2017)

10. Varga, V., Jánosi-Rancz, K.T., Kálmán, B.: Conceptual design of document NoSQL database with formal concept analysis. Acta Polytech. Hungarica **13**(2), 229–248 (2016)

An Integrated Approach for Column-Oriented Database Application Evolution Using Conceptual Models

Pablo Suárez-Otero[1]([⊠]), Michael J. Mior[2], María José Suárez-Cabal[1], and Javier Tuya[1]

[1] University of Oviedo, Gijón, Spain
{suarezgpablo,cabal,tuya}@uniovi.es
[2] Rochester Institute of Technology, Rochester, NY, USA
mmior@cs.rit.edu

Abstract. Schema design for NoSQL column-oriented database applications follows a query-driven strategy where each table satisfies a query that will be executed by the client application. This strategy usually implies that the schema is denormalized as the same information can be queried several times in different ways, leading to data duplication in the database. Because the schema does not provide information such as where the data is duplicated or the relationships between conceptual entities, developers must use additional information when evolving the database. One strategy for accessing this information is to use a conceptual model that must be synchronized and kept consistent with the physical schema. In this work, we propose evolving a column-oriented database application after a schema change with a combination of methods that consists of four sequential stages: 1) reflect the schema change in the conceptual model, 2) take the necessary actions in the schema to maintain consistency between the new conceptual model and the schema, 3) maintain data integrity through migration of data and 4) update and adapt the client application to the new schema.

Keywords: Evolution · Column-oriented database · Data integrity · Program repair

1 Introduction

The design of a database is based on both the requirements of applications and the characteristics of the DBMS. For instance, the schema of a relational database is designed based on the data that will be stored, with emphasis on producing a normalized model. On other hand, schema design for NoSQL databases follows different strategies based on how the data is expected to be used by applications that modify and display the data. For instance, column-oriented databases follow a query-driven approach to schema design to achieve high performance when executing queries, where each table commonly satisfies a query of the client application.

© Springer Nature Switzerland AG 2021
I. Reinhartz-Berger and S. Sadiq (Eds.): ER 2021 Workshops, LNCS 13012, pp. 26–32, 2021.
https://doi.org/10.1007/978-3-030-88358-4_3

This query-driven approach implies a denormalized model as the same information can be queried several times in different ways. This leads to the storage of the same information in different tables of the database. Therefore, evolution of a schema that changes a particular table or column might affect other parts of the database where the same information is stored. Failure to apply the required changes to the rest of the database may result in problems regarding consistency, increasing the risk of columns storing incorrect data instead of the data that they were intended to store.

In relational databases, where the schema is usually normalized, each table stores the information of a single entity or relationship, so the schema is very similar to the conceptual model. Due to this, a common practice is to evolve the database directly via changing the schema. However, in NoSQL databases, and particularly in a column-oriented database, evolution of the schema requires more information. If a developer evolves one of these databases only considering the information provided by the schema, they risk committing mistakes during this evolution because of the lack of relevant information such as how and where the data is duplicated or the relationships that exist between conceptual entities.

This information can be provided by a conceptual model [3, 7] that, in order to remain useful, must always be synchronized with the schema. An incorrect evolution of the database may affect this synchronization by having database structures that contradict the conceptual model, also provoking issues related to data integrity. Client applications are also affected, as they may contain bugs caused by this incorrect evolution, such as code referring to entities that are either not considered in the schema or have different properties. There also have been approaches to infer a conceptual model from the database schema [1, 2], helping the evolution of database schemas that had been designed without employing a conceptual model.

To properly evolve a column-oriented database application from a change in the schema, we propose a collection of methods where each one solves a particular issue using conceptual models. These methods will determine the actions required to keep the conceptual model and the schema synchronized, the data integrity of the database and the database client applications updated to the current version of the schema.

The remainder of this paper is structured as follows. Section 2 contains motivation for this work based on a real scenario. Section 3 details the combination of methods and Sect. 4 contains the conclusion and future work.

2   Motivation

We have studied the evolution of the schema in several open-source projects that use column-oriented databases to store their data [10]. One of these projects is PowSybl[1], which is a framework for real and simulated power systems that has had 35 schema versions during its lifetime. In prior work [10] we focused on issues caused by an incorrect evolution of the database due to lack of consideration of additional information contained in the conceptual model, such as where data are duplicated.

---

[1] https://github.com/powsybl/powsybl-network-store.

One of the identified changes that is prone to cause these issues is the addition of a new column. In the PowSybl project, there was a version[2] where 15 tables were modified by adding the same two columns to each of them, "bus" and "connectableBus", which store information of a new entity named "BusBreaker" and relationships between it and other entities. The week following this evolution, a bug was detected and reported to the developers of the project, warning about an issue related to the schema, which did not have the database structures required to store relationships between "BusBreaker" and "DanglingLine". The developers of PowSybl fixed this bug[3] by adding the columns "bus" and "connectableBus" to a table that was not part of the original 15 tables. As NoSQL column-oriented database applications are focused on storing big data, a mistake like this one can imply the loss of great amounts of data, as all the insertions of relationships between instances of "BusBreaker" and "DanglingLine" would be lost during that week. This scenario is illustrated in Fig. 1.

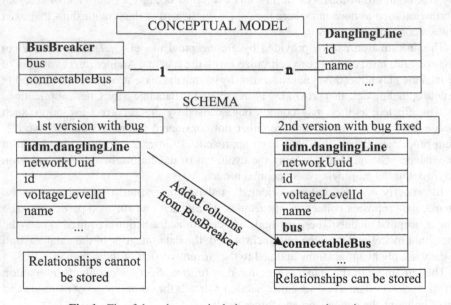

Fig. 1. Fix of the schema to include a new conceptual requirement

The addition of a new column can result from several possible scenarios from a conceptual point of view such as a new conceptual entity, a new relationship, or new attributes. Depending on the type of the change in the conceptual model, developers must perform a specific set of actions to evolve the database, which might involve performing changes in other tables and columns from the schema, data migrations, and changes in the applications that work with the database. Our objective in this paper is

---

[2] https://github.com/powsybl/powsybl-network-store/blob/3c962d5c8f78f56c7be6e7729be2a2 ca910c2bcf/network-store-server/src/main/resources/iidm.cql.

[3] https://github.com/powsybl/powsybl-network-store/blob/49a2745c43b510cd89ada8de9950e1 b33e3c8e2e/network-store-server/src/main/resources/iidm.cql.

to help developers avoid problems related to the evolution of column-oriented database applications when there is a change in the schema by using more information in addition to the schema. In the next section, we propose a combination of methods that uses a conceptual model synchronized with the schema that provides the required information to evolve the database and avoid mistakes.

3 Evolution Procedure

We propose a procedure to evolve the schema that starts with a change in the database structures of the schema and uses a conceptual model that is synchronized with the schema. For this synchronization to be useful, inter-model consistency must be maintained, which assures that the conceptual model is a normalized version of the schema.

The initial information required for the proposed procedure are the current conceptual model, the current schema, a mapping between conceptual model and schema and the change in the schema that triggers this procedure. This procedure is composed of four stages that are illustrated in Fig. 2 along with their interactions with each other. Each stage resolves a particular issue through specific steps:

1. Change the conceptual model to maintain the inter-model consistency:

    1.1. Determine the changes in the conceptual model required to reflect the change in the schema.
    1.2. Apply the changes determined in 1.1 to the conceptual model.

2. Change the schema to maintain the inter-model consistency:

    2.1. Determine the changes in the rest of the schema required to maintain inter-model consistency with the new conceptual model obtained in 1.
    2.2. Apply the modifications from 2.1.

3. Migrate the required data to the created or modified database structures to maintain data integrity:

    3.1. Determine tables that might exhibit data integrity problems.
    3.2. Determine the migration of data required to maintain data integrity, identifying the tables from where to get the data.
    3.3. Execute the migrations determined in 3.2.

4. Update the client application database statements to the new schema:

    4.1. Identify the code and database statements that need to be updated.
    4.2. Modify the queries and code of the client application identified in 4.1.

In the following paragraphs we describe each stage in detail, detailing their objective and the methods that we propose to use in them.

Stage 1 aims to maintain inter-model consistency after a change to the schema by performing the required updates to the conceptual model to reflect the change in the schema. We propose using existing work that studies the renormalization of the schema in a normalized conceptual model [8, 9]. These works propose generating a normalized conceptual model based on a column-oriented schema. We use past work focused on column-oriented databases [8] as a guideline for determining the specific changes to be performed in the conceptual model for each change in the schema.

Stage 2 aims to regain inter-model consistency by applying in the required changes to schema in order to adapt it to the conceptual model generated in stage 1. For instance, an update to the cardinality of a relationship needs to be replicated to every table that stores the relationship. In past work [10], we defined a method which, given a conceptual model, provides the instructions required to reflect the change in the schema. Due to being focused on evolution, we propose using this method for stage 2. To complete the scenarios to cover, we will also use the ones focused on designing a column-oriented database schema from a conceptual model and the queries that are going to be executed by the client application [3, 4, 7].

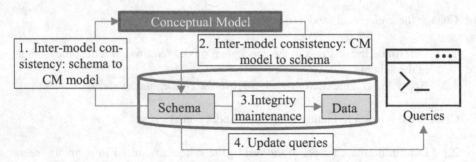

Fig. 2. Full evolution of the database procedure

When the change in the schema does not modify the conceptual model, stages 1 and 2 are skipped. For instance, there could be a new table that satisfies a query that retrieves information already defined in the conceptual model. In this case however, there could be problems related to data integrity, so stages 3 and 4 are still required.

Stage 3 aims to maintain the data integrity of the database. This integrity is jeopardized due to data duplication caused by the denormalization of the schema, as data needs to be kept consistent. To address this problem, we will use a combination of several methods. To identify the scenarios where migrations of data are required to maintain the data integrity after the change in the schema, we will use the method defined in [10], which describes the specific migrations required for each schema change type. The identification of the source tables to get the data to be migrated will be based on the method defined in [11], where we used conceptual models to address an automatic maintenance of the data integrity in scenarios where it was jeopardized. The migration of data process will be performed following the previously defined strategies [6] in order to achieve the best performance possible during the migration process.

The objective of stage 4 is to update the client application by adapting it to the new schema. Although there is no existing work that studies this specific problem, program repair approaches [5] are an interesting option. These approaches aim to fix a bug or solve an inconsistency in software. We propose using a similar approach that updates the application in both the database statements that are embedded in the application and the application code that prepares the database statements and process the result of the execution of these database statements.

4   Conclusion and Future Work

The incorrect evolution of a database causes important problems like data loss or the creation of inconsistencies between the schema and the conceptual view of the data system, which were shown in a real-world scenario. In this work, we proposed a combination of methods that perform the complete evolution of a column-oriented database application after a change in the schema, approaching the schema, the conceptual model, data integrity and client applications. To the best of our knowledge, this is the first work that approaches the evolution of column-oriented database applications in all stages. At the moment, we have developed the solutions for the maintenance of the inter-model consistency from changes in the conceptual to the schema, as well as the identification of the data migrations required to maintain the data integrity.

As future work, we intend to focus on stages whose methods either need to be adapted or that have yet to be developed. For stage 1 we intend to adapt previous work [8] to orientate it for schema evolution. For stage 4 we plan to develop a new method based on program repair is able to update a client application for the new schema. Finally, we aim to automate the process by integrating all methods, connecting the outputs of each stage with the input of the following one.

Acknowledgments. This work was supported by the TestBUS project (PID2019-105455GB-C32) of the Ministry of Science and Innovation, Spain and the TESTEAMOS project (TIN2016-76956-C3-1-R) of the Ministry of Economy and Competitiveness, Spain.

References

1. Abdelhedi, F., Brahim, A.A., Ferhat, R.T., Zurfluh, G.: Reverse engineering approach for NoSQL databases. In: Song, M., Song, I.Y., Kotsis, G., Tjoa, A.M., Khalil, I. (eds.) Big Data Analytics and Knowledge Discovery. DaWaK 2020. Lecture Notes in Computer Science, vol. 12393, pp. 60–69. Springer, Cham (2020). https://doi.org/10.1007/978-3-030-59065-9_6
2. Akoka, J., Comyn-Wattiau, I.: Roundtrip engineering of NoSQL databases. Enterp. Model. Inf. Syst. Archit. **13**, 281–292 (2018)
3. Chebotko, A., Kashlev, A., Andrey, L., Lu, S.: A big data modeling methodology for Apache Cassandra. In: 2015 IEEE International Congress on Big Data, pp. 238–245 (2015)
4. de la Vega, A., García-Saiz, D., Blanco, C., Zorrilla, M., Sánchez, P.: Mortadelo: automatic generation of NoSQL stores from platform-independent data models. Futur. Gener. Comput. Syst. **105**, 455–474 (2020)

5. Gopinath, D., Khurshid, S., Saha, D., Chandra, S.: Data-guided repair of selection statements. In: Proceedings of 36th International Conference on Software Engineering, pp. 243–253 (2014)
6. Hillenbrand, A., Störl, U., Levchenko, M., Nabiyev, S., Klettke, M.: Towards self-adapting data migration in the context of schema evolution in NoSQL databases. In: 2020 IEEE 36th International Conference on Data Engineering Workshops, pp. 133–138 (2020)
7. Mior, M.J., Salem, K., Aboulnaga, A., Liu, R.: NoSE: schema design for NoSQL applications. IEEE Trans. Knowl. Data Eng. **29**(10), 2275–2289 (2017)
8. Mior, M.J., Salem, K.: Renormalization of NoSQL database schemas. In: Trujillo, J., et al. (eds.) Conceptual Modeling. ER 2018. Lecture Notes in Computer Science, vol. 11157, pp. 479–487. Springer, Cham (2018). https://doi.org/10.1007/978-3-030-00847-5_34
9. Ruiz, D.S., Morales, S.F., Molina, J.G.: Inferring versioned schemas from NoSQL databases and its applications. In: Johannesson, P., Lee, M., Liddle, S., Opdahl, A., Pastor López, Ó. (eds.) Conceptual Modeling. ER 2015. Lecture Notes in Computer Science, vol. 9381, pp. 467–480. Springer, Cham (2015). https://doi.org/10.1007/978-3-319-25264-3_35
10. Suárez-Otero, P., Mior, M.J., Suárez-Cabal, M.J., Tuya, J.: Maintaining NoSQL database quality during conceptual model evolution. In: 2020 IEEE International Conference on Big Data (Big Data), pp. 2043–2048 (2020)
11. Suárez-Otero, P., Suárez-Cabal, M.J., Tuya, J.: Leveraging conceptual data models to ensure the integrity of Cassandra databases. J. Web Eng. **18**(6), 257–286 (2019)

Athena: A Database-Independent Schema Definition Language

Alberto Hernández Chillón(✉) ⓘ, Diego Sevilla Ruiz ⓘ,
and Jesús García Molina ⓘ

Faculty of Computer Science, University of Murcia, Murcia, Spain
{alberto.hernandez1,dsevilla,jmolina}@um.es

Abstract. While relational databases are still predominant, there is a growing interest in NoSQL, and many database systems are evolving to accommodate several NoSQL paradigms. Moreover, polyglot persistence is envisioned as the database architecture of complex modern applications. In this heterogeneous scenario, the existence of a paradigm-independent language to specify schemas is of paramount importance. Here we present Athena, a database-independent schema declaration language. Athena is a textual domain specific language based on a generic metamodel able of representing NoSQL and relational schemas. Along this paper, we will describe the requirements of the language, constructs, and some applications of Athena.

Keywords: NoSQL databases · Schema declaration · Unified NoSQL metamodel · Domain specific language

1 Introduction

Widespread adoption of NoSQL systems requires providing developers with existing database utilities for relational systems, such as data modeling tools, as noted in [2]. When building them, the variety of NoSQL data models arises as the main challenge: they should support multiple data models, at least the most popular NoSQL paradigms (columnar, document, graph, and key-value) jointly with the relational model. As far as we know, the Hackolade[1] data modeling tool is the only one offering such multi-model support.

Unified or generic metamodels (e.g., ER) are commonly used to tackle the construction of multi-model tools. Such metamodels are defined with the purpose of representing schemas of different data models in the same format. A unified metamodel for NoSQL and relational databases is presented in [5], where several applications are shown. This metamodel, named U-Schema, was mainly

---

[1] https://hackolade.com/.

This work has been funded by the Spanish Ministry of Science, Innovation and Universities (project grant TIN2017-86853-P).

I. Reinhartz-Berger and S. Sadiq (Eds.): ER 2021 Workshops, LNCS 13012, pp. 33–42, 2021.
https://doi.org/10.1007/978-3-030-88358-4_4

conceived to represent schemas inferred from schemaless NoSQL stores. In this paper, we present the Athena schema declaration language, which is defined on U-Schema, that allows database-independent schemas to be specified. Athena is part of a family of textual domain specific languages (DSL) aimed at performing several kinds of utilities on databases, such as synthetic data generation, and schema evolution [6,7]. These languages can be used as an environment to perform testing on databases (e.g., measuring query and schema operations performance).

Some previous efforts have been made to define languages to specify platform-independent schemas, for example GraphQL and Apache Avro, but they are not designed to declare database schemas. As far as we know, the Typhon project[2] and the Hackolade tool provide the only languages with the same purpose as Athena. However, Athena is based on a unified metamodel, which includes a richer set of abstractions (e.g., structural variations, references, and relationship types). Moreover, Athena offers mechanisms for reusing and composing schemas, as well as syntactic sugar to ease writing schemas: defining types with incomplete information and restrictions, working with a large number of variations, declaring properties without type, among others.

This paper is organized as follows: First, the U-Schema is briefly described. Next, Athena is presented: requirements, language constructs and mechanisms, and implementation. Then, we show current applications for Athena. Finally, Athena is contrasted with similar languages, and some conclusions and future works are outlined.

2   U-Schema: A Unified Data Model

Unified or generic data models are usually proposed to represent schemas of different data models in a uniform format. They are useful to build multi-model tools or heterogeneous database systems. With a uniform format, the implementation effort to implement some utilities such as migrators or database management tools can be significantly reduced.

U-Schema is a unified logical model able to integrate the aforementioned NoSQL data models and the relational model [5]. More significant features of U-Schema are the following: (i) It distinguishes between entity types and relationship types. (ii) It includes the notion of *structural variation* of a type, as data of the same type can be stored with different structure in schemaless NoSQL stores. (iii) It provides three kinds of relationships between types: aggregation, reference, and inheritance. (iv) It allows the definition of *union schema types*, formed by the set of features that result of the union of the features of all its variations. Each feature can be labeled as required or optional depending on whether they are present or not in all the variations. In Fig. 1 the U-Schema metamodel is shown. This metamodel will be briefly described.

A U-Schema model is composed of a set of types (SchemaType) that may be entity types (EntityType) or relationship types (RelationshipType). Schema

---

[2] https://www.typhon-project.org/.

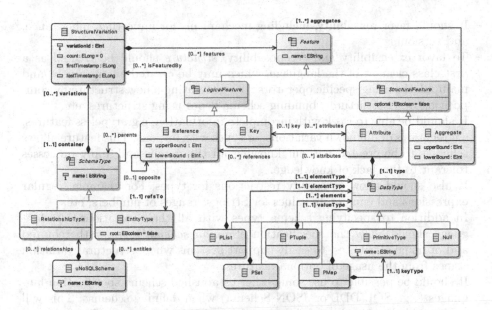

Fig. 1. The U-Schema metamodel.

types have one or more structural variations (StructuralVariation), and they can form a type hierarchy (parent relationship). A StructuralVariation is characterized by a set of features. *Structural* features may be Attributes and Aggregates, and *logical* features may be Keys and References to other objects. Each attribute has a name and a Primitive type (e.g., Number, String, Boolean), or a Collection type (sets, maps, lists, and tuples). An aggregation has a name, a cardinality, and refers to the structural variation or variations it aggregates. A key represents a set of attributes that act as key for an entity type, while a reference refers to an entity type (via refsTo), and it may have its own attributes in case the schema represented is a graph.

3 The Athena Language

3.1 Requirements

While obtaining U-Schema schemas from existing databases is automatically performed by discovery tools, as discussed in [5], when designing schemas, or changing existing ones, for instance to perform certain tests or generate data [7], a language to easily manipulate them is needed. Athena has been designed as a DSL to tackle this need by fulfilling the following requirements:

- The language should be *complete*, that is, it should allow to specify every element of the U-Schema data model. It should also adhere to the principle of least-surprise.

- It should favor reusability, including mechanisms for importing, inheritance, and versioning.
- To favor extensibility and composability, *structure* should be treated as a first class element of the language, which may be created anonymously, and manipulated using specific operators, i.e., generating a new structure by compositing other structures, building schema types using structures, etc.
- It should be able to work with incomplete information, e.g., typeless features, aggregations of unknown variations, or types with options. This feature allows schemas to be created without knowing all the details and apply processes tolerant to this lack of knowledge.
- It also should allow to specify restrictions for types. For example, regular expressions and enumerate values for Strings, ranges of numbers, etc.
- In addition to specifying schema types with all their variations, the language should allow the specification of *union schema types*, with required and optional attributes, to easily support systems where structural variation comes from the usage of optional features.
- It should be possible to use some other established schema specification languages (e.g., SQL DDL or JSON Schema) when defining schemas. This will enhance the integration of Athena with existing languages. The language should be open to be integrated with other languages in the future.

3.2   Syntax and Semantics

An Athena schema declaration is organized in three parts: A header specifying the schema name, an optional set of import statements, and a set of type definitions. Figure 2 shows an Athena schema that will be used as a running example.

Schema Identifiers. Several mechanisms of the language, such as schema importing and versioning, require to assign an identifier to schemas. A schema `identifier` is composed of a name and a version number, which are separated by a colon. The version number allows the evolution of a schema to be tracked over time. It is initialized to 1, and it will be incremented as new schema versions are generated. In the running example, the schema is named *Social_Network* and it is in its first version.

Importing Schemas. Schemas can be imported using their identifier. When declaring a schema, all the types of the imported schemas can be directly used. Figure 3 shows a schema that imports *Social_Network:1* and declares an entity type *Movie* with a feature referencing *Social_Network:1.User*.

Schema Types. A schema is formed by a set of `Entity types` and `Relationship types` as indicated in Sect. 2. Both schema types are composed by a set of features. In addition, the `Feature Set` construct is provided to group

```
Schema Social_Network:1

FSet Timestamp_features {
 created_time:          Timestamp,
 last_activity_date: Timestamp
}

FSet Vote_features {
 upvotes:        Integer ( 0..1000 ),
 downvotes:      Integer ( 0..1000 )
}

Root entity User {
 Common {
  + id:      Identifier,
  ! email: String /^.+@.+\\.com$/,
  type:      String in
             ( "Guest", "User", "Admin"
             ),
  user_data: Aggr<User_data>&
 }
 Variation 1
 {is_active: Boolean}
 Variation 2
 {suspended_acc:Option<Integer,
         Boolean>}
}

Entity User_data {
 address:     String,
 name:        String /^[A-Z][a-z]*$/,
 ? about_me: String
}
```

```
Root entity Comment
 SQL CREATE TABLE Comment
 (
  id VARCHAR(255) NOT NULL,
  message VARCHAR(255) NOT NULL,
  post_id VARCHAR(255) NOT NULL,
  user_id VARCHAR(255) NOT NULL,
  FOREIGN KEY ( post_id )
    REFERENCES Post ( id ),
  FOREIGN KEY ( user_id )
    REFERENCES User ( id ),
  PRIMARY KEY ( id )
 );
 + Timestamp_features
 + Vote_features

Root entity Post
 {
  + id:      Identifier,
  message: String,
  social:
  {
   views:     Integer,
   reactions: Integer,
   shares:    Number
  },
  title:   String,
  user_id: Ref<User>&,
  ? tags:  List<String>
 } U Timestamp_features
  U Vote_features
```

Fig. 2. *Social Network* schema defined using Athena.

features with the purpose of being reused in the definition of other types. In the running example, four entity types are defined: *User, Comment, Post,* and *User_Data.* The former three specify root entities, while the latter specifies an aggregate type used to declare a feature of *User.* Also, the schema includes two feature sets (*FSet*) named *Timestamp_features* and *Vote_features.*

When a schema type has more than one variation, each one of them must be explicitly declared, as shown in the *User* entity type of the running example. Instead of specifying variations, a schema type can also be defined as a *union schema type* by providing a set of features labeled as required or optional. In the running example, *Post* is a *union schema type*, with *tags* as an optional feature.

```
Schema Movie_Friends:1
Import Social_Network:1

Root entity Movie
{
 + id:   Identifier,
 viewers: Ref<Social_Network:1.User>+
}
```

```
Root entity Friend::Social_Network:1.
  User
{
 friends:         Ref<Friend>+,
 favouriteMovies: Ref<Movie>+
}
```

Fig. 3. *Movie Friends* example importing the *Social Network* schema.

Inheritance Mechanism. The language also provides a type inheritance mechanism, which allows to establish a *child-parent* relationship between types. Each feature defined in the parent type will be included in the child type. In Fig. 3, an inheritance relationship exists between the *Friend* entity type and *Social_Network:1.User*.

Features. When declaring features, some qualifiers can be specified to denote the feature is a key (+), optional (?) or restricted to unique values (!). A feature is declared by a name and a type, and the type is not mandatory. A type can denote an `Aggregation`, a `Reference`, a scalar data type, a nested type that will be transformed into an aggregate type, or an array of types. In Fig. 2, the *Post.user_id* feature references *User*, and *User.user_data* aggregates *User_data*. The multiplicities are expressed as + for *one to many*, * for *zero to many*, ? for *zero to one*, and & for one to one.

In addition to the types described above, the language includes the following types: (i) Primitive types can be simple scalar types such as `String` and `Integer`, or specific types that will be system-dependent once a schema is translated to a specific database, such as `Identifier`. (ii) Collection types that can be `Map`, `List`, `Tuple` and `Set`, and (iii) A union type of scalar types (`Option` types), e.g., *User.2.suspended_acc:Option<Integer,Boolean>* in the running example.

When declaring features of some scalar types, ranges and regular expressions can be used to restrict the possible values, as in *User.email* or *User_data.name* where regular expressions are needed, in *User.type* where only certain values are allowed, or in *Vote_features.upvotes* and *Vote_features.downvotes* where integer values need to be on a certain range.

Structures. Athena allows the definition of `structures` in order to ease type definitions. A structure is defined by means of an `expression`. A set of structure operators has been defined to create structures as a composition of others, such as *union*, *intersection*, and *difference*. Each operand may be a schema type, a variation, a feature set or a SQL statement. For example, in Fig. 2, the structures of *Comment* and *Post* are formed by adding their own structure to the structure of *Timestamp_features* and *Vote_features*, and in *Comment* a SQL statement is used as an structure.

3.3   Implementation

Athena has been implemented using the Xtext workbench[3]. First, an abstract syntax was defined for the language in form of an Ecore metamodel [9]. Then, the notation or concrete syntax was defined as a Xtext grammar. Xtext engine automatically generated the editor, parser, and model injector. A translational approach was applied to define the semantics: Athena models are transformed to U-Schema models, and then utilities can be built for Athena, as those introduced in the following section.

---

[3] https://www.eclipse.org/Xtext/.

4   Applications of Athena

Athena may be useful in any tool or utility that requires users to declare schemas not tied to a particular database or data model. Although most NoSQL stores are schemaless, developers need schemas to design databases, as noted by Pascal Desmarets [3], and schemas inferred from data or code must be textually or graphically visualized to be understood. Next, we will briefly expose how Athena can be applied in three different scenarios: (i) Generating schemas, (ii) Evolving schemas, and (iii) Generating synthetic data. These three scenarios are illustrated in Fig. 4.

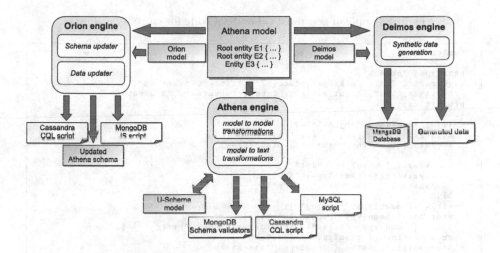

Fig. 4. A schematic view of the main applications of Athena.

Generating Schemas

The Athena engine is able to generate specific code for certain databases by using *model to text* (*m2t*) transformations. For databases with explicit schemas like Cassandra or MySQL, a *CQL* or *SQL* script is generated. In Fig. 5, the code generated for Cassandra and MySQL to create the *Post* entity type from the *Social_Network* schema is shown. On the other hand, for schemaless databases such as MongoDB, a JSON Schema validation script can be provided. In Fig. 6, the validator generated for entity type *Post* is shown.

Also, U-Schema models can be transformed into an Athena schema and vice versa by means of a *model to model* (*m2m*) transformation. In this way, U-Schema models may be textually visualized and Athena schemas can be used as an input to U-Schema tooling.

```
CREATE TABLE IF NOT EXISTS Post   CREATE TABLE Post (
(                                  id VARCHAR(255) NOT NULL,
                                   message VARCHAR(255) NOT NULL,
  id uuid,                         social INTEGER NOT NULL,
  message text,                    title VARCHAR(255) NOT NULL,
  social Social,                   user_id VARCHAR(255) NOT NULL,
  title text,                      created_time TIMESTAMP NOT NULL,
  user_id uuid,                    last_activity_date TIMESTAMP NOT NULL,
  tags list<text>,                 upvotes INTEGER CHECK
  created_time timestamp,            ( upvotes BETWEEN 0 AND 1000 ) NOT NULL,
  last_activity_date timestamp,    downvotes INTEGER CHECK
  upvotes int,                       ( downvotes BETWEEN 0 AND 1000 ) NOT NULL,
  downvotes int,                   FOREIGN KEY (user_id) REFERENCES User (id),
  PRIMARY KEY (id)                 FOREIGN KEY (social) REFERENCES Social (id),
                                   PRIMARY KEY (id)
);                                 );
```

Fig. 5. Example of generated cql and sql code for entity type *Post*.

```
$jsonSchema:
{
  bsonType: "object",
  required: [ "id", "message", "social", "title", "user_id",
    "created_time", "last_activity_date", "upvotes", "downvotes" ],
  properties:
  {
    id: { bsonType: "objectId" },
    message: { bsonType: "string" },
    social: { bsonType: "object", properties:
    {
        views: { bsonType: "int" },
        reactions: { bsonType: "int" },
        shares: { bsonType: "number" }
    }},
    title: { bsonType: "string" },
    user_id: { bsonType: "objectId" },
    tags: { bsonType: "array", items: { bsonType: "string" } },
    created_time: { bsonType: "timestamp" },
    last_activity_date: { bsonType: "timestamp" },
    upvotes: { bsonType: "int", minimum: 0, maximum: 1000 },
    downvotes: { bsonType: "int", minimum: 0, maximum: 1000 }
  }
}
```

Fig. 6. Example of a Javascript validator generated for entity type *Post*.

Evolving Schemas

Orion is a DSL that implements a taxonomy of schema changes [6]. An Orion
script is composed of a sequence of operations to be applied on an Athena schema
given as an input. As a result of this process the Orion engine outputs, as can be
seen in Fig. 4, the following artifacts: (i) An updated Athena schema, and (ii) A
set of scripts able to migrate data for a specific database system. The output
schema will have evolved according to the specified Orion operations, and thus
this new schema will have the same name as the input schema, but with an
incremented version number.

Generating Synthetic Data

Deimos is a declarative DSL aimed to generate synthetic data [7]. The generation of synthetic datasets requires a schema declaration. A Deimos specification is composed of a set of data generation rules and mappings that bind those rules to Athena schema elements. As shown in Fig. 4, the Deimos engine takes an Athena schema and a Deimos specification and generates datasets of synthetic data. The generated content may be injected directly into a database, or stored in files elsewhere. During this process the Athena schema does not change.

5 Related Work

Several languages have been created to declare schemas in a platform-independent way. With the exception of TyphonML [8], the purpose of the rest of the languages is not to declare database schemas. In this section, we will contrast Athena with some of the most relevant of these languages.

Typhon is an H2020 European project aimed to provide support to work with polystores. Within this project, the TyphonML language has been defined to express schemas and schema operations for NoSQL and relational schemas. Each TyphonML declaration includes the logical schema (with entities and relationships among them) and mappings from logical elements to elements of a particular database. Next, we remark the main differences between Athena and TyphonML: (i) Both languages allow schemas to be declared in an abstract way, but they differ in the requirements: TyphonML is aimed to specify schemas in a polyglot persistence scenario; We have designed Athena to specify schemas in an environment of database testing, among other applications, as shown in the previous section. (ii) We have applied *concern separation* to have a family of languages in which each language is tailored to a specific database concern. At this moment, these concerns are schema specification, schema operations, and database population. (iii) Athena is based on a unified metamodel. (iv) Athena provides a richer set of constructs than TyphonML, which facilitate schema reuse and agility to creators, e.g., importation mechanism, embedding SQL declarations, and incomplete information. (v) Athena includes mechanisms to handle structural variations.

GraphQL [1] is an alternative to the REST architecture in building client-server applications. With GraphQL, first, data schema are defined, and then queries can be issued on APIs. Both schemas and queries are not tied to any specific database, and schemas are used to validate queries. A schema is a set of types that specify root objects. The properties of a data type can be scalar data, collections (arrays and lists), and nested objects. Unions and enumerated types are also supported. Athena and GraphQL have clearly been designed with different purposes, which is evidenced in the mechanisms provided for both languages. Beyond the definition of data types (entity and relationship types in Athena), both languages have nothing else in common. The differences noted above would also be applicable in the case of GraphQL.

JSON Schema [4] also allows data schemas to be declared. It could be convenient for semi-structured data (e.g., schemas of document stores), but the lack of subtyping and references makes it difficult to specify schemas for other data models as graph or relational. In addition, structural variation is not considered, and the schema declarations are verbose because flexibility and agility were not taken into account as requirements.

6 Conclusions and Future Work

In this paper, we have introduced a DSL aimed to declare database-independent schemas. We have shown how the language fulfills the elicited requirements, as completeness and reusability. Also, the usefulness of the language has been illustrated by showing three application cases.

Our future work includes: (i) Supporting other schema specification languages (e.g., JSON Schema) to declare structures. (ii) Defining additional restrictions over types. (iii) Implementing generators for other NoSQL stores, such as Neo4j for graphs and Redis for key-value. And (iv) Exploring the possibility of adding extension points to Athena with the purpose of easing the language extensibility.

The full implementation of Athena, as well as a complete specification of the language with examples of installation and usage may be found at the following webpage https://catedrasaes-umu.github.io/NoSQLDataEngineering/tools.html.

References

1. GraphQL Webpage. https://graphql.org/. Accessed July 2021
2. Bacvanski, V., Roe, C.: Insights into NoSQL Modeling: A Dataversity Report (2015)
3. Desmarets, P.: NoSQL Data Modelling in Practice (2020). invited talk at CoMoNoS Workshop
4. Droettboom, M., et al.: Understanding JSON Schema. Release 7.0 (2020)
5. Fernández Candel, C., Sevilla Ruiz, D., García Molina, J.: A Unified Metamodel for NoSQL and Relational Databases. CoRR abs/2105.06494 (2021). https://arxiv.org/abs/2105.06494
6. Hernández Chillón, A., Sevilla Ruiz, D., García Molina, J.: Towards a taxonomy of schema changes for nosql databases: the Orion language. In: ER 2021, 40th International Conference on Conceptual Modeling (ER). St. John's, NL, Canada (October 2021)
7. Hernández Chillon, A., Sevilla Ruiz, D., Garcia-Molina, J.: Deimos: a model-based NoSQL data generation language. In: CoMoNoS Workshop in Conceptual Modeling International Conference (2020)
8. Kolovos, D.S., et al.: Domain-specific languages for the design, deployment and manipulation of heterogeneous databases. In: 2019 IEEE/ACM 11th International Workshop on Modelling in Software Engineering (MiSE), pp. 89–92 (2019)
9. Steinberg, D., Budinsky, F., Paternostro, M., Merks, E.: EMF: Eclipse Modeling Framework 2.0. Addison-Wesley Professional, Boston (2009)

Empirical Methods in Conceptual Modeling (EmpER) 2021

EmpER 2021 Preface

Conceptual modeling continues to be a subject of intense study with important applications in diverse fields ranging from software engineering and business to biology and law. The development and sharing of conceptual models have long been understood to support important human activities such as communication, design, reasoning, decision-making, and documentation. A great variety of languages, frameworks, tools, and techniques are continuously being proposed to aid effective development and use of practical conceptual models. The success of such contributions, however, depends on whether their merits can be demonstrated in practice, i.e., whether they indeed help practicing model producers and model users in achieving their goals. At the same time, production and use of conceptual models gives rise to psychological, social, organizational, and other contextual phenomena that deserve to be studied if we are to understand how conceptual modeling is applied in practice.

The 4th International Workshop on Empirical Methods in Conceptual Modeling (EmpER 2021), co-located with the 40th International Conference on Conceptual Modeling (ER 2021), aimed at bringing together researchers with an interest in the empirical investigation of conceptual modeling. Like its three predecessors, the fourth installment of the workshop invited three kinds of papers: full study papers describing a completed study, work-in-progress papers describing a planned study or study in progress, and position, vision and lessons learned papers about the use of empirical methods for conceptual modeling. The workshop particularly welcomed negative results as well as proposed empirical studies that are in their design stage so that authors can benefit from early feedback and adjust their designs prior to real data collection. A total of 20 reviewers were invited to serve the Program Commitee of the workshop based on their record of past contributions in the area of empirical conceptual modeling.

Overall, a total of three papers were accepted out of the six that were reviewed. The accepted papers include a reference framework for articulating conceptual modeling research (Delcambre et al.), a study of enriched ontologies for intergenerational family reconstitution from historical records (Embley et al.), and an exploration of how artificial intelligence (AI) can support domain conceptualization (Feltus et al.). The workshop involved presentations of the papers followed by discussion and audience feedback to the authors. A keynote presentation was offered by Oscar Pastor of the Universidad Politécnica de Valencia, Spain.

October 2021

João Araujo
Dominik Bork
Miguel Goulão
Sotirios Liaskos

Articulating Conceptual Modeling
Research Contributions

Lois M. L. Delcambre[1], Stephen W. Liddle[2(✉)], Oscar Pastor[3],
and Veda C. Storey[4]

[1] Portland State University, Portland, OR, USA
lmd@pdx.edu
[2] Brigham Young University, Provo, UT, USA
liddle@byu.edu
[3] Universitat Politècnica de València, Valencia, Spain
opastor@dsic.upv.es
[4] Georgia State University, Atlanta, GA, USA
vstorey@gsu.edu

Abstract. To contribute to the ongoing discussions related to understanding and organizing the field of conceptual modeling, this paper
presents a reference framework for articulating conceptual modeling
research. The framework accommodates the diverse nature of conceptual modeling research contributions. The framework can describe many
styles of research, including empirical research. The framework was
inspired by, and is able to characterize, a large set of published papers
in conceptual modeling. The framework allows researchers and reviewers
to acknowledge the contributions of their work. Using the framework to
describe a research paper also promotes meaningful discussion among
reviewers and readers.

Keywords: Conceptual modeling research contributions · Context for
conceptual modeling · Framework for conceptual modeling research

1 Introduction

Recent efforts to characterize conceptual modeling, from a number of perspectives, share several goals: define the field; articulate the depth and breadth of
the field; advance the field; promote the impact of the field (beyond the conceptual modeling community); and express a shared understanding of the field.
The objective of this paper is to provide a mechanism to characterize research
contributions in the field of conceptual modeling (CM) based on the many, and
varied, types of contributions that appear in the literature. In addition, our aim
is to promote discussion among those attempting to understand a paper (e.g.,
reviewers). Although there is no single generally accepted definition of "conceptual modeling," our goal is not to present yet another definition of conceptual
modeling. Rather, we distill the essence of diverse existing definitions to recognize and discuss various conceptual modeling research contributions.

© Springer Nature Switzerland AG 2021
I. Reinhartz-Berger and S. Sadiq (Eds.): ER 2021 Workshops, LNCS 13012, pp. 45–60, 2021.
https://doi.org/10.1007/978-3-030-88358-4_5

2   Related Work

A significant number of interesting efforts seek to understand and assess the state of the art of conceptual modeling. Guarino et al. [15] examine the fundamental notion of a conceptual model by characterizing conceptual models with respect to conceptual semantics and ontological commitments. A number of requirements that can enable a representation to qualify as a conceptual model are discussed, based on questions such as: What are the main characteristics of conceptual models? What makes them different from other models? How can one assess that a given model is a good one? Similarly, Mayr and Thalheim [25] study the "anatomy" of conceptual models and their characteristics to clearly distinguish different types of conceptual models. In their work on this anatomy, they identify the need to have a definition or at least a set of criteria to describe the nature of conceptual modeling and delimit the semantics of the term "conceptual model".

While the main intention of these works is to present a "signature" of conceptual modeling to categorize conceptual modeling, our goal is different. We do not discuss what is, or what is not, a conceptual model. For example, we do not debate whether the relational data model is conceptual. Rather, we acknowledge different interpretations concerning which CM characteristics should be considered to decide whether a given model should be considered conceptual. Assuming that conceptual modeling can have different interpretations for different authors, we focus on how to characterize a research result that is presented as a conceptual modeling contribution by providing clear and concrete criteria to compare, analyze, and discuss the "signature" of the research contribution itself.

Our goal is to provide a precise conceptual framework to identify the intended research contribution (e.g., as pertaining to a model, metamodel, or model instance). This characterization could support an author's belief that their published work, as published in the literature, provides a relevant result in CM terms. Our framework enables an author or reviewer to delimit the conceptual modeling context of a research work and then focus on the type of contribution provided, either by characterizing the relevant artifact itself (e.g. a model, conceptual modeling language, metamodel, or notation) or its practical context of use (e.g. a method, process, tool, or algorithm).

In Delcambre et al. [6] we introduced a reference framework for conceptual modeling itself. This paper, in contrast, focuses specifically on conceptual modeling research, refining our approach in [7]. The new framework integrates the knowledge and experience accumulated during the continued evolution and application of our framework.

Other recent papers focus on characterizing the field of conceptual modeling. Jaakkola and Thalheim [18] examine the progression of data models and their role in information systems development, highlighting the importance of modeling. Lima et al. [23] trace the evolution of conceptual models over four decades to identify emerging areas of interest. Härer and Fill [16] investigate the evolution of research topics related to conceptual modeling based on a bibliometric analysis of conceptual modeling research; their two major observations are that topics were related to the technical aspects of modeling and to business processes.

Our research is open in the sense that it can be used to describe results coming from various research efforts that might not be considered as pure conceptual modeling research.

3   The Framework

In a workshop that we conducted at ER 2017, leading researchers in the field broadly agreed that a conceptual model must represent what someone has in their mind for a domain; that is, someone's conceptualization of a domain [6]. There are likely additional uses for conceptual models such as specifying executable representations of a system, but we embrace the notion that a CM is used for human purposes of communication, discussion, negotiation, and so forth.

Any research contribution in conceptual modeling must involve some kind of model, language, or other representation that is used as a conceptual model. We can characterize other aspects of this representation, such as the types of human users who may create or use the representation, what their goals are, what they are trying to capture in the representation, the level of abstraction at which they are working, and so forth. Fundamentally, though, a research contribution in conceptual modeling is necessarily associated with a representation that is properly viewed as a conceptual model of something.

We have observed three significant and distinct types of research contributions: those centered on a model, language, metamodel, representation, or notation for CM (thus exploring "what" is being represented); those centered on a method, process, tool, or algorithm for a CM-related purpose (thus examining "how" representations can be used); and those that contribute CM vision, philosophy, principles, or a review (thus encompassing a variety of CM representations in a high-level way). In this paper we reference these three types by the first word of each description: *model*, *method*, and *vision*, respectively.

One example of a *model* contribution is Chen's classic paper [3] where he proposed the ER model and notation. A more recent example is Vallecillo and Gogolla's ER 2020 paper [29] proposing a way to specify dynamic deontic constraints using UML and OCL. *Model* contributions are numerous in the literature. *Method* contributions propose or reason about processes, methods, tools, or algorithms in the context of conceptual modeling. A recent example is Link's ER 2020 paper [24] that formally characterizes the implication problem associated with Neo4j keys and presents an algorithm to decide the implication problem. *Method* contributions are also plentiful. *Vision* contributions may describe a general vision for some aspect of CM, discuss philosophical issues surrounding CM or CMR, or survey some aspect of the field. Our paper is an example of this type; others include Lima et al. [23] and Härer and Fill [16].

We now present our proposed framework as Fig. 1 shows. The first section of the framework (collapsed in Fig. 1) identifies the work being characterized by specifying standard bibliographic information (title, authors, citation details).[1]

---

[1] See https://blondie.byu.edu/ccmr for a prototype of the web form; this prototype only demonstrates the form, not back-end storage of filled-out forms.

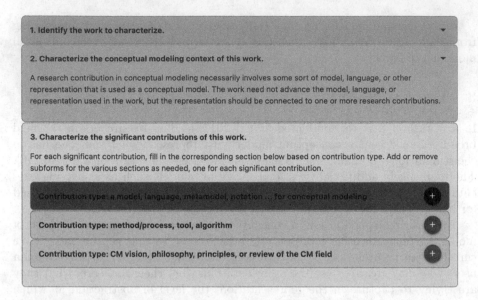

Fig. 1. Overview of the framework for articulating CMR contributions.

The second section of the framework describes the CM context for the work, as Fig. 2 shows. To qualify as a contribution in conceptual modeling, there must exist a representation that is used as the conceptual model associated with the contribution. We characterize the representation along three dimensions: (1) Which groups of users are likely to use this representation? (2) What are the users capturing as they use this representation? (3) What is the level of abstraction at which the users are working as they use this representation? These answers place the contribution in a context that allows it to be understood and compared or contrasted with other contributions. In Fig. 2 we supply sample controlled vocabularies based on our experience in the CM field (as researchers and practitioners) and on our extensive review of CM papers as described below. These vocabularies are not exhaustive; all questions permit free-text answers.

Context tends to be less distinguishing for *vision* contributions than it is for *model* or *method* contributions. So, for example, a survey paper such as Härer and Fill's [16] works in the context of all representations, users, and kinds of things represented across all levels of abstraction as used in the surveyed literature.

3.1   Characterizing Research Contributions

As Fig. 3 shows, we characterize *model* contributions by identifying the associated artifact, highlighting contribution types from a controlled vocabulary of possibilities, and describing the contribution in narrative. As before, the controlled vocabulary is not intended to be exhaustive.

Similarly, Fig. 4 shows how we characterize *method* contributions by listing the artifact, characterizing its purpose, and describing its significance. The additional question asks the purpose of *method* contributions, because a method or an algorithm is designed to perform some function, and is helpful to express the

2. Characterize the conceptual modeling context of this work.   ▲

A research contribution in conceptual modeling necessarily involves some sort of model, language, or other representation that is used as a conceptual model. The work need not advance the model, language, or representation used in the work, but the representation should be connected to one or more research contributions.

List the representation used/treated as a conceptual model in this work	Representation

Which groups of users are likely to create, modify, read, or otherwise use this representation?	☐ Philosophers
	☐ Foundational ontology developers or conceptual modeling language developers
	☐ Stakeholders, domain experts (e.g. business experts, AI application experts), requirements developers
	☐ Software, database, or knowledge representation designers
	☐ Software, database, or knowledge representation implementors
	☐ Software, database, or knowledge representation system performance specialists
	☐ Other

Describe (optional)

What is captured in this representation?	☐ Data (e.g. database, data warehouse, dataspace, data lake, ...)
	☐ Processes (e.g. business processes, goals, preferences, priorities, ...)
	☐ Scenarios, events, agents
	☐ Interactions (e.g. among human users and automated components, ...)
	☐ Knowledge, rules, "smart" systems
	☐ Other

Describe (optional)

What is the level of abstraction for this representation?	☐ Computation-independent
	☐ Platform-independent
	☐ Platform-specific
	☐ Other

Describe (optional)

Fig. 2. Context section of the proposed framework.

goal of the underlying activity. Note that empirical research techniques can be described using the framework, e.g. to evaluate or compare models or methods.

Figure 5 shows the template for characterizing *vision* contributions with a brief description of the contribution and a selection from a small, controlled vocabulary of contribution categories, e.g. vision papers, discussion of philosophical issues, discussion of principles related to CM, and broad surveys.

A publication may make multiple significant contributions of the same or different type(s), each of which should be identified. The "+" icon in each section gives the user of our prototype the ability to add an additional subsection.

4   Evaluating the Framework

We describe our initial efforts to evaluate whether the components of our framework are useful and, collectively, provide broad coverage for the field of conceptual modeling research.

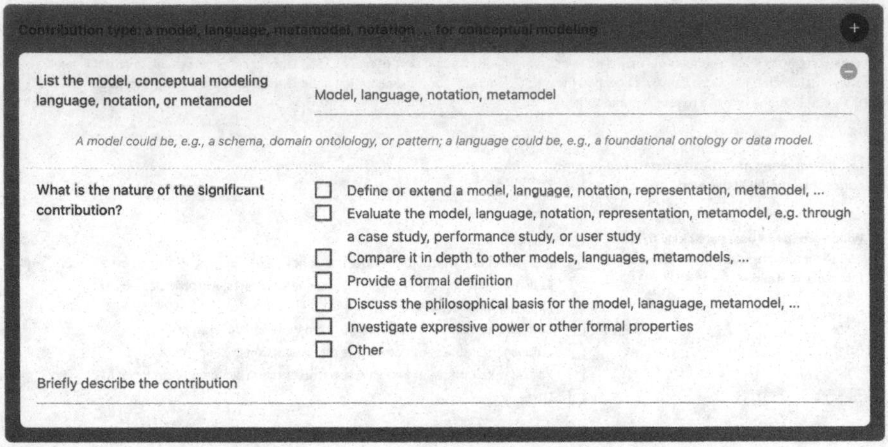
Contribution type: a model, language, metamodel, notation ... for conceptual modeling

List the model, conceptual modeling language, notation, or metamodel — Model, language, notation, metamodel

A model could be, e.g., a schema, domain ontolology, or pattern; a language could be, e.g., a foundational ontology or data model.

What is the nature of the significant contribution?

- ☐ Define or extend a model, language, notation, representation, metamodel, ...
- ☐ Evaluate the model, language, notation, representation, metamodel, e.g. through a case study, performance study, or user study
- ☐ Compare it in depth to other models, languages, metamodels, ...
- ☐ Provide a formal definition
- ☐ Discuss the philosophical basis for the model, lanaguage, metamodel, ...
- ☐ Investigate expressive power or other formal properties
- ☐ Other

Briefly describe the contribution

Fig. 3. Section for describing *model* contributions.

4.1 Evaluating Framework Components

Since our work is focused on research contributions in CM, an initial step was to systematically outline the main research contributions of all long and short papers in the ER 2019 proceedings [22]. In order to be representative, we used the entire proceedings. The types of contributions are summarized in Table 1. 16 papers contributed a conceptual model/language/representation/notation/metamodel, 18 papers contributed a method/tool/algorithm for CM, and 8 papers contributed both. The 2019 proceedings also included one high-level, vision paper. The left column of Table 1 provides a general indication of the topic of the contribution: 10 papers contributed domain-specific conceptual models (called reference ontologies, patterns, etc.). Approximately half of the papers contributed a conceptual modeling language (or foundational ontology) or a DB schema definition language. Other papers contributed requirements languages and tools, searching or querying conceptual model data, plus two others.

Table 1. Papers in the ER 2019 proceedings [22].

Topic	Count	Type of contribution			
		Model	*Method*	*Model & Method*	*Vision*
(Domain-specific) CM	10	7	0	3	0
CML, DB schema language	21	7	10	3	1
Requirements	5	2	3	0	0
Search/query	5	0	3	2	0
Other	2	0	2	0	0
Total	**43**	**16**	**18**	**8**	**1**

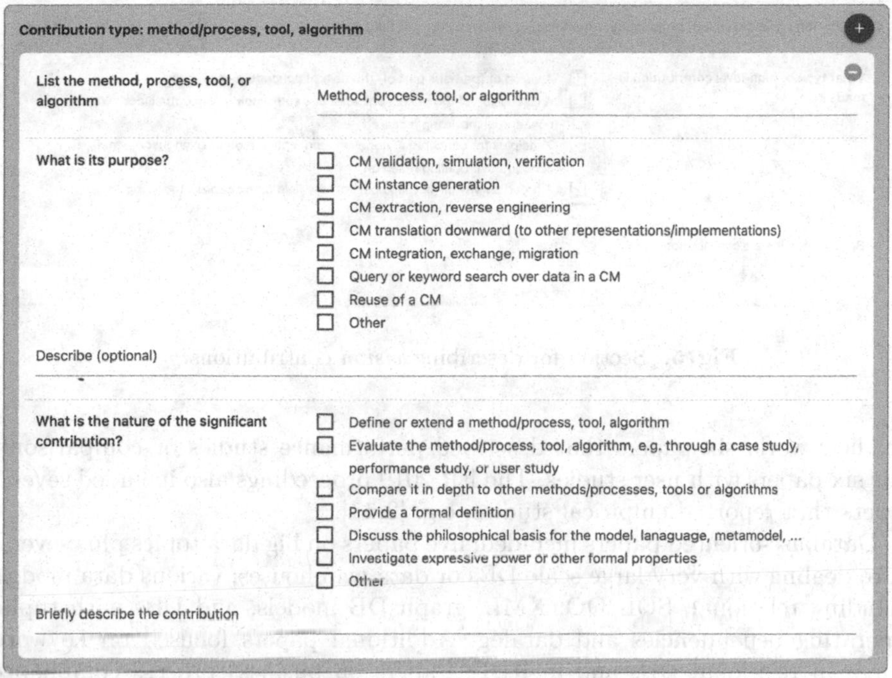

Fig. 4. Section for describing *method* contributions.

The domain-specific contributions covered a broad range of domains, including: OO programming language concepts, DB tuning concepts, data graph for taxi rides, data constitution in geology, genomics, railway interlocking systems, online market places, smart contracts, and a requirements pattern. The collection included five papers contributing or evaluating algorithms, ten papers offering case studies or use case scenarios, several papers with formal definitions of CM or query languages or papers that investigated formal properties of such languages, a number of papers that provided in-depth ontological foundations

Table 2. Range of user types in ER 2019 papers.

User type	Count
BP people	4
CM designers	7
DB designers/DB integration people	7
Performance specialists	5
Requirements developers	7
Users who search/query	5
Other	8
Total	43

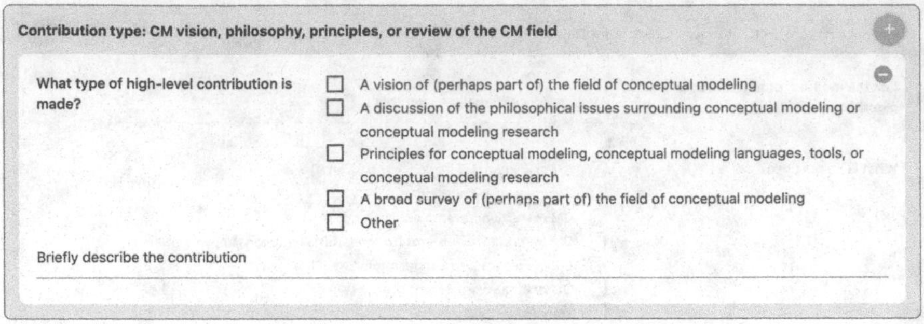

Fig. 5. Section for describing *vision* contributions.

for their work, six papers that described performance studies or comparisons, plus six papers with user studies. The ER 2019 proceedings also included several papers that reported empirical studies, e.g. [2,11].

Database-oriented papers included: five papers on big data topics plus several more dealing with very large scale DBs or data warehouses; various data models including relational, SQL/OO, XML, graph DB models; and DBs with tuple-generating dependencies and datalog. Additional papers focused on keyword search in relational DBs and in RDF. Papers on business process compliance included constraints on business processes and goal modeling. Finally, there were papers on requirements for various kinds of systems.

Table 2 provides a window into the CM context by showing the range of user types that could be identified in various papers. The "other" category includes user types that were present in just one paper. In general, our framework is able to describe this range of papers, suggesting that it can provide reasonable coverage for the field of CM research, including empirical studies. This also supports our decision to be flexible in what we consider a conceptual model. Various aspects of the framework are utilized in a variety of ways. This indicates that all of the elements of the framework appear to be useful.

4.2   Evaluating Use of the Framework

Our first exercise involved all of us using the framework to evaluate eight papers from the 2019 ER proceedings [1,5,10,13,14,17,21,27], selected because they cover a diverse set of topics as described above. Our second exercise used papers from the ER 2020 proceedings [9]. We randomly selected one long paper from each of the conference sessions and then randomly selected three more.

Multiple Characterizations of Papers from ER 2019. We were interested in whether multiple reviewers would come to agreement when applying the framework to a paper. Table 3 provides a list of papers reviewed. In every case, the discussion of these characterizations led to agreement. We discuss several of these papers here.

Table 3. Overview of characterization of papers from ER 2019 [22].

Paper	# Rev.	Contribution type	Reviewer agreement
[27]	4	*Model*	Strong agreement
[21]	4	*Model*	
[14]	3	*Model*	
[5]	3	*Model & method*	Strong agreement (primary and secondary)
[10]	4	*Model & method*	Strong agreement: different choices for contribution, secondary contribution
[17]	3	*Model* (one reviewer also described it as *method*)	Strong agreement: different choices for contribution; minority view led to better understanding
[13]	4	*Model & method*	
[1]	4	*Model & method*	

Our review of the first paper in Table 3 [27] demonstrated agreement but with different levels of specificity and details. "What is captured in the representation ..." included: "knowledge/rules (how to perform value ascriptions when making decisions prior to action—based on agents' beliefs", "CM expressed in UFO", "ontology of beliefs, value ascriptions, value experiences" and, simply, "goals". "Who are intended users ...?" responses included: "stakeholders, domain experts", "KiP (knowledge-intensive process) agents (e.g., business experts, experts in AI applications)", "planners/managers of knowledge intensive processes". Every reviewer selected *model* with different details as Table 4 shows. Such differences (e.g. in specificity) are to be expected and do not indicate disagreement about the research in the paper.

Table 4. Primary research contribution of [27].

Description of contribution
CM of decision-making in Knowledge-intensive processes
Knowledge-intensive Process ontological notions of different categories of beliefs (motivating, cost, incompatibility, etc.)
Common ontology on value and risk; used to present ontology of value experiences and goals
Ontologically-supported value-oriented CM in the form of a well-founded ontology
[The authors] defined or extended CM to define decision-making in knowledge-intensive processes based on value and risk ascriptions and goal processing theories
[The paper] defines a well-founded ontology to characterize and structure the ontological nature of the relationships between mental states of participating agents and their goals
[The authors] defined/extended the CM; provided examples/case studies

A paper with essentially perfect agreement among the reviewers was the third paper in Table 3 [14]. Table 5 shows how the main research contribution was described by various reviewers for the fifth paper in Table 3 [10]. Some reviewers emphasized the representation (the cache signatures) while others emphasized

Table 5. Primary research contribution of [10].

Model	Method
MapReduce with code signatures for jobs in the query plan	An algorithm/method for improving efficiency of the tuning phase of job development (one reviewer's choice for main contribution)
Defined/extended MapReduce job with code signatures/job similarity – to recycle tuning setups	(Second/minor contribution) details not given for the matching algorithm for the code signature cache; maybe main contribution is automated process that uses cache matching algorithm

the algorithm for matching cache signatures—a key part of the tool that would use the signatures. These reviews easily supported our discussion of the paper and indeed the differences between reviewers led to a more comprehensive understanding of the paper's contributions. Thus the outcome was within expectations and supported our goals.

For the next-to-last paper in Table 3 [13], one reviewer regarded it as contributing a method for modeling data lakes and data marts to support data science; the other reviewers viewed it as contributing/evaluating Data Vault for modeling data lakes. This is an example of where an initial disagreement led to an interesting discussion and, finally, a rich interpretation of the paper's contribution. The last paper in Table 3 [1] showed another example of disagreement that led to discussion and then deeper understanding (see Table 6). Most of the reviewers described a *model* contribution. The collective set of reviewers offered a more complete picture of the contribution. One reviewer described it as a *method* contribution as shown in the right column. This description was in concert with the other reviewers but suggested a broader contribution as a new method.

Multiple Characterizations of Papers from ER 2020. When we characterized the first six randomly selected, long papers from ER 2020 [4,12,19,20,28,31], we artificially limited ourselves to identifying the single most important research contribution of each paper. This helped us better focus on using the framework with precision. Then, we randomly selected three more long papers from ER 2020 [8,16,26] and removed the restriction in order to identify multiple contributions where applicable. Table 7 contains an overview of our review of these papers. We discuss a few of these papers below.

The first paper in Table 7 [20] had near perfect agreement for the two reviewers. Similarly, there was very strong agreement on the primary research contribution for the second paper [12]. The fifth paper in Table 7 [26] demonstrates very strong agreement on the essence of the paper. The seventh paper [31] showed strong agreement but from different perspectives. One reviewer emphasized method and the other emphasized the tool. The next-to-last paper in

Table 6. Primary research contribution of [1].

Model	Method
Railway interlocking system (RIS) domain-specific model (UML class diagram-based)	One reviewer wrote: they contributed a methodology for formal specification of relay-based railway interconnect systems using B-method, CM-based ontology supported semantic enrichment (for the purpose of the method) covering environmental and safety concerns
Domain-specific CM for railway interlocking systems; they defined this CM which consists of electrical components and system environment; provided formal specification of the CM	
The Dysfunctional Analysis Ontology was used to analyze state dependency between electrical components (past work) to describe environmental dependencies (novel)	
Goal-oriented requirements ontology: specification is putatively improved by incorporating environmental sources of risk	

Table 7 [4] showed perhaps our most interesting (initial) disagreement with these two descriptions of the main research contribution: "authors evaluated 3 different CMs/notations for integrating business rules with business processes" vs. "authors investigated user behavior in dual artifact tasks (business processes and business rules)". Our in-depth discussion led to both reviewers being able to recognize the additional contribution missing from their original review. The final paper in Table 7 [16] was a high-level paper with a bibliometric analysis of published CM papers and venues along with content analysis.

We observe that there can be substantial (and even essentially full) agreement without identical entries in the framework fields for a paper. Note that this is why free-text description is important for describing the main contribution. It allows reviewers to express what they see as the contribution and promotes discussion among reviewers. Rather than fostering perfect agreement, the framework should aid discussion and help different reviewers reach a better understanding of a paper's research contributions by providing a systematic outline of aspects to consider. As expected, we observed this outcome repeatedly across our several evaluation experiments.

Table 7. Overview of characterization of papers from ER 2020.

Paper	# Rev.	Contribution type	Reviewer agreement
[20]	2	*Method*	Strong agreement
[12]	3	*Model*	Strong agreement
[19]	2	*Model*	Strong agreement
[28]	2	*Method*	Strong agreement
[26]	4	*Model* (1), *method* (1), *model & method* (2)	Strong agreement
[8]	4	*Model*	Strong agreement
[31]	2	*Method*	Strong agreement; different perspectives
[4]	2	*Method* (1), *model* (1)	Led to interesting discussion; broadened appreciation for the paper; resulted in agreement
[16]	4	*vision*	Strong agreement: reviewers highlighted different aspects; led to a broader appreciation of the paper

4.3 Discussion

In our initial work on characterizing CM research [7], we presented an earlier version of our framework and posited that we could assist with searching CM literature in a repository where papers had been characterized using the framework, in addition to the goals of articulating research contributions and promoting discussion of research contributions and directions. The context section of the earlier framework was influenced by our previous work on characterizing conceptual modeling [6]. Although our earlier work demonstrated coverage and utility of the components in our framework, there was much diversity in how the context section was used, and systematic differences in how the research contributions were described [7].

As we adjusted our framework, we simplified and shifted the emphasis of the CM context section to draw the reviewer's attention to the representation that serves as a CM associated with the research described in the paper. We ask the reviewer to identify the type of user who would create, view, discuss, negotiate, or otherwise use that representation. The context section of the framework now serves as the basis for discussing whether a paper is relevant to CM. The context section of the framework was used consistently throughout our reviews with one exception: the field for intended level of abstraction, which uses standard MDA language.

Second, we simplified the section of the framework for model contributions. Our earlier framework [7] had separate rows for (domain-specific) CM contributions, ideal models or patterns, conceptual modeling language contributions, and metamodel contributions. Given that there is active debate in the research community regarding distinctions between these categories, this led to some confusion for reviewers as to which row(s) to choose. Since our goals are orthogonal to these distinctions, we allow the reviewer to describe the contribution in a paper within the section entitled "List the model, conceptual modeling language, notation, or metamodel" (see Fig. 3)—without having to choose one of those types and thus without having to enter the debate. We also extended the types of contribution associated with a *model* contribution based in part on the work by Wieringa [30] and all papers in ER 2019. Lastly, we put more emphasis on the free-text description of the significant contribution of the paper.

Similarly, we simplified the process/tool/algorithm section by eliminating the rows for method vs. tool because it is common for a paper that introduces a new algorithm, for example, to also build a tool that uses the algorithm or vice versa. We extended the types of significant contributions exactly as in the previous section and put more emphasis on the free-text description. Finally, we added a third section to describe high-level contributions in CM research, once again, inspired in part by Wieringa [30].

5   Conclusion

This paper has articulated and presented a reference framework for conceptual modeling research that extends prior research on understanding and organizing the field of conceptual modeling, by explicitly recognizing its diverse nature. The intent of the framework is to be a useful mechanism by which researchers can acknowledge and discuss the contributions of their work, and to identify related areas of new research, or extensions to existing efforts. The framework can be seen as a source of inspiration for empirical research intended to identify and characterize CM-based contributions coming from different venues. Indeed, replication of experiments can provide valuable data to compare and articulate CM-based contributions.

Our specific goals for the framework are to: (1) be easy to use for researchers and practitioners; (2) capture the breadth of research contributions in CM; (3) promote meaningful discussion among reviewers and readers in two important tasks of identifying whether a paper is relevant to CM and its significant research contribution(s); and (4) admit a wide variety of types of representations, at different levels of abstraction, as representations that serve as conceptual models. We take a broad interpretation of the many definitions of a conceptual model in the literature, yet require that the representation that serves as a conceptual model must support communication, discussion, and negotiation among human users (in the intended community). The framework identifies the criteria to be measured in a conceptual modeling project, including those that focus on empirical assessments. Our future research will replicate experiments that will apply and evaluate the framework in practice with external participants.

References

1. de Almeida Pereira, D.I., Debbech, S., Perin, M., Bon, P., Collart-Dutilleul, S.: Formal specification of environmental aspects of a railway interlocking system based on a conceptual model. In: Laender, A.H.F., Pernici, B., Lim, E.-P., de Oliveira, J.P.M. (eds.) ER 2019. LNCS, vol. 11788, pp. 338–351. Springer, Cham (2019). https://doi.org/10.1007/978-3-030-33223-5_28
2. Bork, D., Schrüffer, C., Karagiannis, D.: Intuitive understanding of domain-specific modeling languages: proposition and application of an evaluation technique. In: Laender, A.H.F., Pernici, B., Lim, E.-P., de Oliveira, J.P.M. (eds.) ER 2019. LNCS, vol. 11788, pp. 311–319. Springer, Cham (2019). https://doi.org/10.1007/978-3-030-33223-5_26
3. Chen, P.: The entity-relationship model–toward a unified view of data. ACM Trans. Database Syst. **1**(1), 9–36 (1976)
4. Chen, T., Sadiq, S., Indulska, M.: Sensemaking in dual artefact tasks – the case of business process models and business rules. In: Dobbie, G., Frank, U., Kappel, G., Liddle, S.W., Mayr, H.C. (eds.) ER 2020. LNCS, vol. 12400, pp. 105–118. Springer, Cham (2020). https://doi.org/10.1007/978-3-030-62522-1_8
5. Costal, D., Franch, X., López, L., Palomares, C., Quer, C.: On the use of requirement patterns to analyse request for proposal documents. In: Laender, A.H.F., Pernici, B., Lim, E.-P., de Oliveira, J.P.M. (eds.) ER 2019. LNCS, vol. 11788, pp. 549–557. Springer, Cham (2019). https://doi.org/10.1007/978-3-030-33223-5_45
6. Delcambre, L.M.L., Liddle, S.W., Pastor, O., Storey, V.C.: A reference framework for conceptual modeling. In: Trujillo, J.C., et al. (eds.) ER 2018. LNCS, vol. 11157, pp. 27–42. Springer, Cham (2018). https://doi.org/10.1007/978-3-030-00847-5_4
7. Delcambre, L.M.L., Liddle, S.W., Pastor, O., Storey, V.C.: Characterizing conceptual modeling research. In: Panetto, H., Debruyne, C., Hepp, M., Lewis, D., Ardagna, C.A., Meersman, R. (eds.) OTM 2019. LNCS, vol. 11877, pp. 40–57. Springer, Cham (2019). https://doi.org/10.1007/978-3-030-33246-4_3
8. Derave, T., Sales, T.P., Gailly, F., Poels, G.: Towards a reference ontology for digital platforms. In: Dobbie, G., Frank, U., Kappel, G., Liddle, S.W., Mayr, H.C. (eds.) ER 2020. LNCS, vol. 12400, pp. 289–302. Springer, Cham (2020). https://doi.org/10.1007/978-3-030-62522-1_21
9. Dobbie, G., Frank, U., Kappel, G., Liddle, S.W., Mayr, H.C. (eds.): Conceptual Modeling - 39th International Conference, ER 2020, Vienna, Austria, November 3–6, 2020, Proceedings, Lecture Notes in Computer Science, vol. 12400. Springer, Heidelberg (2020)
10. Filho, E.R.L., de Almeida, E.C., Scherzinger, S.: Don't tune twice: reusing tuning setups for SQL-on-hadoop queries. In: Laender, A.H.F., Pernici, B., Lim, E.-P., de Oliveira, J.P.M. (eds.) ER 2019. LNCS, vol. 11788, pp. 93–107. Springer, Cham (2019). https://doi.org/10.1007/978-3-030-33223-5_9
11. Flório, C., Lencastre, M., Pimentel, J., Araujo, J.: iStar-p: a modelling language for requirements prioritization. In: Laender, A.H.F., Pernici, B., Lim, E.-P., de Oliveira, J.P.M. (eds.) ER 2019. LNCS, vol. 11788, pp. 540–548. Springer, Cham (2019). https://doi.org/10.1007/978-3-030-33223-5_44
12. Gianotti, M., Riccardi, F., Cosentino, G., Garzotto, F., Matera, M.: Modeling interactive smart spaces. In: Dobbie, G., Frank, U., Kappel, G., Liddle, S.W., Mayr, H.C. (eds.) ER 2020. LNCS, vol. 12400, pp. 403–417. Springer, Cham (2020). https://doi.org/10.1007/978-3-030-62522-1_30

13. Giebler, C., Gröger, C., Hoos, E., Schwarz, H., Mitschang, B.: Modeling data lakes with data vault: practical experiences, assessment, and lessons learned. In: Laender, A.H.F., Pernici, B., Lim, E.-P., de Oliveira, J.P.M. (eds.) ER 2019. LNCS, vol. 11788, pp. 63–77. Springer, Cham (2019). https://doi.org/10.1007/978-3-030-33223-5_7

14. Gonçalves, E., Araujo, J., Castro, J.: iStar4RationalAgents: modeling requirements of multi-agent systems with rational agents. In: Laender, A.H.F., Pernici, B., Lim, E.-P., de Oliveira, J.P.M. (eds.) ER 2019. LNCS, vol. 11788, pp. 558–566. Springer, Cham (2019). https://doi.org/10.1007/978-3-030-33223-5_46

15. Guarino, N., Guizzardi, G., Mylopoulos, J.: On the philosophical foundations of conceptual models. Inf. Modell. Knowl. Bases **31**(321), 1 (2020)

16. Härer, F., Fill, H.-G.: Past trends and future prospects in conceptual modeling - a bibliometric analysis. In: Dobbie, G., Frank, U., Kappel, G., Liddle, S.W., Mayr, H.C. (eds.) ER 2020. LNCS, vol. 12400, pp. 34–47. Springer, Cham (2020). https://doi.org/10.1007/978-3-030-62522-1_3

17. Holubová, I., Svoboda, M., Lu, J.: Unified management of multi-model data - (vision paper). In: Laender, A.H.F., Pernici, B., Lim, E.-P., de Oliveira, J.P.M. (eds.) ER 2019. LNCS, vol. 11788, pp. 439–447. Springer, Cham (2019). https://doi.org/10.1007/978-3-030-33223-5_36

18. Jaakkola, H., Thalheim, B.: Sixty years-and more-of data modelling. Inf. Modell. Knowl. Bases XXXII **333**, 56 (2021)

19. Johannesson, P., Perjons, E.: An ontological analysis of the notion of treatment. In: Dobbie, G., Frank, U., Kappel, G., Liddle, S.W., Mayr, H.C. (eds.) ER 2020. LNCS, vol. 12400, pp. 303–314. Springer, Cham (2020). https://doi.org/10.1007/978-3-030-62522-1_22

20. Komar, K.S., Santra, A., Bhowmick, S., Chakravarthy, S.: EER→MLN: EER approach for modeling, mapping, and analyzing complex data using multilayer networks (MLNs). In: Dobbie, G., Frank, U., Kappel, G., Liddle, S.W., Mayr, H.C. (eds.) ER 2020. LNCS, vol. 12400, pp. 555–572. Springer, Cham (2020). https://doi.org/10.1007/978-3-030-62522-1_41

21. Kuehnel, S., Trang, S.T.-N., Lindner, S.: Conceptualization, design, and implementation of EconBPC – a software artifact for the economic analysis of business process compliance. In: Laender, A.H.F., Pernici, B., Lim, E.-P., de Oliveira, J.P.M. (eds.) ER 2019. LNCS, vol. 11788, pp. 378–386. Springer, Cham (2019). https://doi.org/10.1007/978-3-030-33223-5_31

22. Laender, A.H.F., Pernici, B., Lim, E., de Oliveira, J.P.M. (eds.): Conceptual Modeling - 38th International Conference, ER 2019, Salvador, Brazil, November 4–7, 2019, Proceedings, Lecture Notes in Computer Science, vol. 11788. Springer, Heidelberg (2019)

23. Lima, L.H.C., Laender, A.H., Moro, M.M., de Oliveira, J.P.M.: An analysis of the collaboration network of the international conference on conceptual modeling at the age of 40. Data Knowl. Eng. **130**, 101866 (2020)

24. Link, S.: Neo4j keys. In: Dobbie, G., Frank, U., Kappel, G., Liddle, S.W., Mayr, H.C. (eds.) ER 2020. LNCS, vol. 12400, pp. 19–33. Springer, Cham (2020). https://doi.org/10.1007/978-3-030-62522-1_2

25. Mayr, H.C., Thalheim, B.: The triptych of conceptual modeling. Softw. Syst. Model. **20**(1), 7–24 (2020). https://doi.org/10.1007/s10270-020-00836-z

26. Pérez-Soler, S., Guerra, E., de Lara, J.: Model-driven chatbot development. In: Dobbie, G., Frank, U., Kappel, G., Liddle, S.W., Mayr, H.C. (eds.) ER 2020. LNCS, vol. 12400, pp. 207–222. Springer, Cham (2020). https://doi.org/10.1007/978-3-030-62522-1_15

27. Richetti, P.H.P., Baião, F.A., Campos, M.L.M.: Decision-making in knowledge-intensive processes: the case of value ascription and goal processing. In: Laender, A.H.F., Pernici, B., Lim, E.-P., de Oliveira, J.P.M. (eds.) ER 2019. LNCS, vol. 11788, pp. 363–377. Springer, Cham (2019). https://doi.org/10.1007/978-3-030-33223-5_30

28. Timmerman, Y., Bronselaer, A., De Tré, G.: Quantifying the impact of EER modeling on relational database success: an experimental investigation. In: Dobbie, G., Frank, U., Kappel, G., Liddle, S.W., Mayr, H.C. (eds.) ER 2020. LNCS, vol. 12400, pp. 487–500. Springer, Cham (2020). https://doi.org/10.1007/978-3-030-62522-1_36

29. Vallecillo, A., Gogolla, M.: Modeling behavioral deontic constraints using UML and OCL. In: Dobbie, G., Frank, U., Kappel, G., Liddle, S.W., Mayr, H.C. (eds.) ER 2020. LNCS, vol. 12400, pp. 134–148. Springer, Cham (2020). https://doi.org/10.1007/978-3-030-62522-1_10

30. Wieringa, R.J., Maiden, N.A.M., Mead, N.R., Rolland, C.: Requirements engineering paper classification and evaluation criteria: a proposal and a discussion. Requir. Eng. 11(1), 102–107 (2006)

31. Winter, K., van der Aa, H., Rinderle-Ma, S., Weidlich, M.: Assessing the compliance of business process models with regulatory documents. In: Dobbie, G., Frank, U., Kappel, G., Liddle, S.W., Mayr, H.C. (eds.) ER 2020. LNCS, vol. 12400, pp. 189–203. Springer, Cham (2020). https://doi.org/10.1007/978-3-030-62522-1_14

Inter-Generational Family Reconstitution with Enriched Ontologies

David W. Embley[1,2], Stephen W. Liddle[1(✉)], Deryle W. Lonsdale[1], and Scott N. Woodfield[1,2]

[1] Brigham Young University, Provo, UT, USA
{embley,woodfiel}@cs.byu.edu, {liddle,lonz}@byu.edu
[2] FamilySearch International, Lehi, UT, USA

Abstract. Enriching ontologies can measurably enhance research in digital curation. We support this claim by using an enriched ontology to address a well known, challenging problem: record linkage of historical records for intergenerational family reconstitution. An enriched ontology enables extraction of birth, death, and marriage records via linguistic grounding, curation of record-comprising information with pragmatic constraints and cultural normatives, and record linkage by evidential reasoning. The result is an automatic and highly accurate reconstruction of family trees. Empirical evidence shows that conceptual modeling theory can be applied to important real-world problems and yield excellent results.

Keywords: Record linkage · Enriched ontologies · Linguistic grounding · Pragmatic constraints · Cultural normatives · Evidential reasoning

1 Introduction

Genealogical family relationships often form the basis for digital curation content within a community of interest. Genealogical research focuses on internal family relationships, whereas prosopographical studies focus on external relationships of family members to community services, employment networks, marriages, and social and religious groups. For historical group studies and other applications such as inherited-disease research and assisting genealogy enthusiasts, we show in this paper that augmenting ontologies with rich real-world constraints and cultural normatives can lead to a fully automatic reconstitution of intergenerational family-lineage trees from information automatically extracted from semi-structured records found in community-oriented family history books. Empirical accuracy measurements demonstrate the effectiveness of this automated approach.

Genealogical data is of great interest to individuals and organizations for a variety of reasons, such as performing prosopographical studies, learning about

© Springer Nature Switzerland AG 2021
I. Reinhartz-Berger and S. Sadiq (Eds.): ER 2021 Workshops, LNCS 13012, pp. 61–74, 2021.
https://doi.org/10.1007/978-3-030-88358-4_6

the history of one's own ancestors, or discovering one's genetic heritage. Commercial and nonprofit entities such as Ancestry.com, 23andMe, and FamilySearch International gather and curate this data; governments are also major participants, curating census, transportation, and military service data, among many other types of sources. FAIR principles of data management [15] are helpful in supporting a robust ecosystem, though these principles are currently applied unevenly. Genealogical data exists in a wide variety of formats, from ancient stone carvings to medieval parchment manuscripts, printed books, and modern databases. Photographs and microfilming have been important preservation techniques, and more recently digitization has been especially important in preserving and sharing this data. However, effective search within the vast mountain of genealogical data requires that records be semantically understood and linked accurately according to family relationships.

Figures 1, 2, 3, and 4 show text snippets from family history books. Each mention of a person in a document is a *persona*. The objective is to discover the intergenerational relationships given the *persona records*—the personas and their related information. This requires (1) discovery of parent-child relationships among the personas and (2) discovery of which personas refer to the same person—a persona record linkage problem. Examples:

- In Fig. 1 the persona "Rev. Ezra Stiles Ely" matches the persona "Ezra Stiles Ely" despite their having different spouses and children born 20 years apart. Elsewhere in *The Ely Ancestry* [13] is a persona with birth, death, marriage, and parent-child information fully consistent with Ezra's having the two mentioned wives along with their marriage and death dates that form time windows in which the two children Ben and Harriet were born?
- In Fig. 2 persona "TEEGARDEN, WM. WALTER" matches persona "W.W. TEEGARDEN" despite the name variations.
- In Fig. 3, is the persona "John Adam" who was christened on 30 May 1652 the same as persona "Adam, John" married to Jean Reid? His age when Jean's son John was born would have been about 21—a likely age for a father of a first child. Or, is he the same person as the John Adam who was married to Agnes Andro? A marriage in 1679 would have been when he was about 27—not unreasonable. Or, is he neither of these two?
- In Fig. 4, persona Hans in household B024 is clearly the same persona as Hans Böse in household B025. The information about Hans in B024 references his marriage on 20.10.1704 to his first spouse, Könke Ütjen, in B025.

We call our ontology-enriched record linking system *OntoLink* because of its use of enriched ontologies [12]. Its contributions include:

1. ontology enrichments: linguistic grounding (Sect. 2.1), pragmatic constraints (Sect. 2.2), cultural normatives (Sect. 2.3), and evidential reasoning (Sect. 2.4); and
2. (a) a shallow-match blocking technique that remains efficient but allows for cross-block matches and (b) a deep-match, evidential-reasoning technique that not only successfully matches personas but also yields the reasoning behind matches, mismatches, and low-confidence possible matches (Sect. 3).

243327. Rev. Ben Ezra Stiles Ely, Ottumwa, Ia., b. 1828, son of Rev. Ezra Stiles Ely and Mary Ann Carswell; m. 1848, Elizabeth Eudora McElroy, West Ely, Mo., who was b. 1829, d. 1871, dau. of Abraham McElroy and Mary Ford Radford; m. 2nd, 1873, Abbie Amelia Moore, Harrison, Ill., who was b. 1852, dau. of Porter Moore and Harriet Leonard. Their children:

    1. Elizabeth B., b. 1849.
    2. Ben-Ezra Stiles, b. 1856.
    3. George Everly Montgomery, b. 1858, d. 1877.
    4. Laura Elizabeth, b. 1859.
    5. LaRose DeForest, b. 1861.
    6. Charles Wadsworth, b. 1863.
    7. Mary Anita, b. 1865.
    8. Francis Argyle, b. 1876.

243320. Harriet Clarissima Ely, b. 1848, dau. of Ezra Stiles Ely and Caroline Thompson Holmes; m. Beale Steenberger Blackford, Parkersburg, W. Va. Their children:

    1. Caroline Holmes Ely.

Fig. 1. Text Snippet from *The Ely Ancestry* [13]—family expansion and migration beginning in Boston, Massachusetts, USA (~1650–1900).

2 Ontological Enrichments

The OntoLink pipeline for automatically constructing inter-generational family lineage trees depends critically on the ontological enrichments we propose. It begins with information extraction based on linguistic grounding and proceeds through information curation based on the semantics of pragmatic constraints and cultural normatives which prepares the extracted information for family tree construction via evidential reasoning.

2.1 Linguistic Grounding

A user programs an extraction engine, GreenQQ [4,10], by giving examples. GreenQQ generates templates from given examples to classify entities in a book's text stream. Then, with respect to a chosen "head" class, GreenQQ groups identified entities into records from which OntoLink can generate object and relationship instances that populate the conceptual model underlying an ontology.

For example, from Fig. 3 a user may give GreenQQ the sample text ", 30 May 1652.\n". With the date marked as belonging to the class *ChristeningDate*, GreenQQ generates the template pattern ", ChristeningDate: [NUM1or2 CAP NUM4] . EOL". When applied over the entire book, all text snippets that satisfy this pattern are classified as christening dates. Similarly, templates can be created for birth dates, which (as Fig. 3 shows) follow the lit-

TEEGARDEN, CATHERINE   404 West Fourth St   d 6 May 1941 1:00p.m. Wayne Hosp
    Greenville OH   BD Greenville 8 May 1941   b 20 Nov 1865 Greenville Twp Dke
    Co OH   age 75-5-16   f JOHN SWAC? HERSHEY Lancaster Co PA   m ANNA YOUNG
    Lancaster Co PA   widowed   housewife   sp W.W. TEEGARDEN   physician Dr Gil-
    bert Sayle   religion Evangelical & Reform   funeral 8 May 1941 2:30p.m.
    Thursday Evangelical & Reform   Rev E.V. Louks   survived by 3 sons ROLAND
    Sidney, HAROLD Washington NC, and CHESTER Albany NY, 1 daughter LORENE
    TEEGARDEN Cincinnati

TEEGARDEN, LORENE   d 2 Nov 1946 Washington D.C. residence for 2 years   BD Green-
    ville Cem Greenville OH 5 Nov 1946   single   3 brothers HAROLD of Washing-
    ton D.C., ROLAND of Sidney OH, CHESTER of NY

TEEGARDEN, WM. WALTER   d 6 July 1936 Greenville   BD Greenville 8 July 1936
    b 17 July 1862 Brown Twp Dke Co OH   age 74-11-19   f MOSES TEEGARDEN Dke Co
    OH   m HANNAH DAY MENDENHALL   sp CATHERINE TEEGARDEN

Fig. 2. Three *Miller Funeral Home Records* [9]—patrons of a funeral home in Greenville, Ohio, USA (∼1910–1950).

eral "**born**" and also for the names of the children with birth and christening dates, which have the template pattern "**SOL Name:[CAP], (NUM1or2 — born)**". Then, with "**Name**" chosen as the "head" class, GreenQQ can group classified entities into christening and birth records—hundreds of them in the Kilbarchan book.

GreenQQ record processing also provides for identifying and resolving references to personas like those in Fig. 4. A user can create a template to identify **B025** associated with **Hans** in household **B024** as a reference to his spouse in household **B025**. Then, when forming records, a match on the marriage dates ensures that the correct spouse persona in the household will have been identified.

2.2 Pragmatic Constraints

Pragmatic constraints facilitate a semantic analysis of GreenQQ's syntactically extracted information. In Fig. 1, for example, it is impossible to syntactically associate **Rev. Ely**'s children with their proper mother. Pragmatically, however, **Francis** cannot be a child of **Elizabeth** since she was dead when **Francis** was born. OntoLink identifies and, when possible, rectifies these kinds of errors [16].

For inter-generational family reconstitution, if a potential merge of two personas violates a pragmatic constraint, OntoLink raises a red flag and rejects the merge. If, for example, the parents of two potentially merged personas do not properly correspond, a merge would violate the constraint that a person can have only two parents. In addition to signaling impossibility, violations can also flag improbability. In Fig. 3, for example, a merge of **John Adam** christened on **30 May 1652** and **John Adam** of **Lochwinnoch** would mean that the child **Marion**, christened on **24 Jan. 1662**, would have been born when **John** was only about 10 years old—improbable.

OntoLink also raises red flags when corresponding values such as names and birth dates in potentially matching personas are not close enough to be

Mathew, born 29 June 1752.
Janet, born 26 Nov. 1754.
Elizabeth, born 15 April 1756.
William, 24 Oct. 1760.
Adam, John, in Penall
    Joan, 25 April 1651.
    John, 30 May 1652.
    Isobell, 23 Mar. 1655.
Adam, John, par. of Lochwinnoch
    Marion, 24 Jan. 1662.
Adam, John, and Jean Reid
    John, 14 Nov. 1673.
Adam, John, par., and Agnes Andro in Killellan, in Clavens 1691
                                        m. Killellan 23 Jan. 1679
    Janet, 8 Nov. 1691.
    Mary, 2 April 1693.
Adam, John, and Janet King, in Kilmacolm
    John, June 1683.
Adam, John, in Kirktoun, and Margaret How
    William, 24 Nov. 1689.
    Jean, 13 Mar. 1692.
    Margaret, 8 June 1694.

Fig. 3. *Parish of Kilbarchan* Text Snippet [7]—a community of Scottish worshippers (~1640–1780).

B024
Casten Böse, Brinksitzer, * ca. 1644, □ 11.4.1727, 83 J.,
∞ An N.N., * ca. 1637, □ 6.5.1719, 81 ½ J.,
Kinder: Hans * ca. 1674, ∞I. 20.10.1704, B025
    Rathje * ca. 1660, ∞ Ringstedt 13.6.1682 Gretje Holweges, Köhlen,
    (ziehen nach Kührstedt)

B025
Hans Böse, Brinksitzer, Hs. Nr. 46, * ca. 1674 aus B024, + 10.2.1752, 78 J., in einem Graben ertrunken,
∞I. 20.10.1704 **Könke Ütjen/Itken/Itjen**, (To. Claus Ü., Brinksitzer, nachweisbar 1677), * ca. 1673, + ca. 1715, 42 J.,
Kinder: Casten ~ 25.10.1705, □ 9.11.1705
    Casten ~ 28.1.1707
    Claus ~ 23.9.1710,
∞II. 19.7.1716 **Anne von Soosten**, (verm. To. Johann, nicht Claus v. S., Lintig, wie im KB reg.),
* 6.8.1688, + 12.3.1739,
Kinder: Anne ~ 13.6.1717
    Johann ~ 15.3.1720
    Hinrich ~ 12.2.1723, ∞ 20.10.1746, B027
    Hans ~ 5.3.1726, ∞ 3.12.1756, B028
    Stopher * 17.4.1729, + 5.2.1731
    Mette Alheit * 17.8.1731, ∞ 20.11.1758 Johann Reyels, R033

Fig. 4. Text snippet from *Familienbuch des Kirchspiels Flögeln* record book of families in the Flögeln Parish in Lower Saxony, Germany (~1670–1900).

considered equivalent. In Fig. 1, for example, based on the name, Mary Ann Carswell is clearly not the same person as Caroline Thompson Holmes even though they have the same spouse. On the other hand, W.W. TEEGARDEN in Fig. 2 is the same person as TEEGARDEN, WM. WALTER even though their name parts have different spellings and orderings.

2.3 Cultural Normatives

Information obtained by "reading between the lines" [3] is invaluable in inter-generational family reconstitution. Surnames of the children in Figs. 1 and 3 can be ascertained knowing cultural normatives. Likewise, in Fig. 2 it is clear that TEEGARDEN is CATHERINE's married surname and that her maiden surname is HERSHEY. Reading between the lines, it is also possible to garner missing information. Cultural normatives and local religious practice strongly indicate that John Adam's missing date of birth in Fig. 3 was a few weeks prior to his christening.

To make these cultural normatives easy to work with, OntoLink standardizes the text and canonicalizes the text values. It recasts all dates in the form (day, spelled-out month, year), and it canonicalizes them as Julian date ranges so that, for example, Mary Anita's birth date in Fig. 1 is canonicalized as 1865001-1865365. For locations, OntoLink standardizes by ordering administrative levels as usual and canonicalizes by specifying longitude and latitude. For names, OntoLink standardizes by giving birth names in their usual capitalization and order, and canonicalizes by labeling name parts and including titles, married names, and suffixes. For example, TEEGARDEN, CATHERINE in Fig. 2 is standardized as "Catherine Hershey" and canonicalized as "Title(s): FirstName(s): Catherine BirthSurname: Hershey MarriedSurname(s): Teegarden Suffix(es):". If she were a physician, she might also have the suffix "M.D".

2.4 Evidential Reasoning

Inter-generational family tree construction consists of identifying individuals and establishing spouse and parent-child relationships. Persona records comprise this information but for each individual i the persona records that pertain to i must be identified and merged. Identifying which persona records to merge is a record linkage problem whose resolution requires evidential reasoning.

Automated record linkage has been studied for more than 60 years [11] and continues to be studied with varying degrees of success [1,2,5]. Standard approaches consist of three phases: input preparation, blocking, and within-block matching. OntoLink's ontology enrichments provide the basis for enhancing each phase of record linking: input preparation is more extensive, blocking is governed by shallow matching based largely on inferred evidence, and final matching is deep—based on an extensive use of garnered ontological knowledge.

Input Preparation. As Sects. 2.1, 2.2 and 2.3 describe, OntoLink creates for each persona (each mention instance of a person in a document) a *persona record* consisting of extracted and standardized name, date, and location facts for birth, marriage, and death events and all extracted and inferred "one-hop" family relationships to parents, spouses, and children. Recall, in particular, that for every lexical value there is both a standardized value (to aid identity matching) and a canonical value (to aid in measured closeness matching). Because of its importance in matching, OntoLink also adds an estimated birth date, when possible, for every persona for whom no birth date has been extracted. The estimate is based on (1) any extracted christening, death, burial, and marriage event dates (e.g. an estimated birth date being normally a few weeks before or even right up to the date of christening) or (2) extracted birth dates of one-hop relationships (e.g. a first child being born 20 years or so after a mother's birth). The estimated birth date is then set, marked as approximate, and given a date range. For John Adam in Fig. 3 christened on 30 May 1652, for example, the computed pair is: (estimated birth date: ~1652109, estimated birth date span: 1652067-1652151). If several estimates are possible, the most precise estimate is chosen.

Blocking (Shallow-Match Equivalence Class Construction). OntoLink orders the persona records by description information richness (most to least). Selecting from this list, it forms an ordered list of equivalence classes with each equivalence class also being ordered by persona-record richness. The equivalence-class relationship is: "is a plausible match with the first persona placed in the equivalence class". Thus, in greedy fashion typical of standard blocking, we add each persona record to the first equivalence class to which it has a plausible match with the first persona record. The criteria for being a plausible match are (1) that birth surnames (if any) match within a specified edit distance; that if no surnames, then at least one (if any) of the married surnames match within a specified edit distance; and that the first names weakly correspond (one name sequence subsumes the other, where matching names have the same initial, have an identical initial/first-letter, or have spelled-out or abbreviated names that match within a specified edit distance) and (2) that birth Julian date ranges (extracted or estimated) overlap, or the minimum of the earlier date range to the maximum of the later date range is within five years. Standard blocking techniques normally require that all potential matches appear in the same block. OntoLink's blocking does not, because any persona that does not deep match (as described next) with all the preceding personas in the equivalence class is pushed downstream in the ordered equivalence-class list in such a way as to maintain the invariant constraints of the yet unprocessed part of the shallow equivalence-class list.

Matching (Deep-Match Equivalence Class Construction). The equivalence-class relationship is: "is a match". The check is deep and based on the ideas (1) that if two personas are merged, then the merged persona makes sense semantically and (2) that the evidence for the match is sufficient to yield a high level of certainty. Each persona in a shallow match equivalence class beyond the first is deep-match-checked pairwise against *all* prior personas in the list. This ensures that the match relationship is reflexive, symmetric, and transitive (for those that remain in the equivalence class).

1. **Semantically Reasonable.** A merge of persona P_1 and P_2 is semantically reasonable if (1) neither P_1 nor P_2 individually raises a red flag as explained in Sect. 2.2, (2) combining corresponding known lexical values into a single value raises no red flag, and (3) a (temporary) merge

of P_1 and P_2 raises no red flag. After merging, all non-duplicate person-parent, person-child, and person-spouse relationships of both P_1 and P_2 are added along with one of the two relationships for each duplicate. A relationship is a duplicate if referenced related personas are shallow-equivalent. For example, relationship $Person(P_1)$—$Spouse(P_3)$ is a duplicate of relationship $Person(P_2)$—$Spouse(P_4)$ if persona P_1 shallow-matches persona P_2 and persona P_3 shallow-matches persona P_4. Red flags are raised when pragmatic constraints are violated (e.g. too many parents, children born after their mother's death, overlapping marriages that violate cultural norms).

2. **High-Level of Certainty.** A single red flag rejects a deep match, but the absence of red flags does not confirm a deep match. Constraint-checker-returned probabilities that do not exceed the red-flag threshold can be considered yellow (cautionary) if they tend toward the red-flag threshold and are green (supportive) otherwise. To compute the certainty of a match with no red flags, we invert the probability of a constraint violation for green and yellow flags and determine whether there is enough green-flag evidence to overcome any yellow-flag concerns. OntoLink's particular technique is a variation of the technique described in Lawson et al. [8] into which it injects green- and yellow-flag probabilities. A vector $\langle x_1, ..., x_n \rangle$ is populated with the probability of a match for each lexical attribute and for each name attribute of each person-spouse, person-parent, and person-child relationship (the probability is zero if one or both personas have no value for the attribute). Beforehand, a weight vector $\langle w_1, ..., w_n \rangle$ is established in which each w_i is the weight the ith lexical comparison should carry for determining a positive persona match. The weights are learned over a ground truth of matched personas.[1] The dot product of the probability vector and the weight vector produces a scalar value. Larger values indicate greater confidence in the match. By inspecting proposed matches in our data, we set a threshold that divides the proposed matches into those considered to have a high enough level of certainty to be declared a match and those that do not.

Examples: In the Kilbarchan text snippet in Fig. 3 in a run of OntoLink, some of the John Adam personas shallow match, but none deep match. In the Miller text snippet in Fig. 2, OntoLink matches the CATHERINE TEEGARDEN personas and matches the two mentions of her husband. The LORENE personas shallow match but (incorrectly) fail to deep match. They match because her brothers align, but OntoLink only considers one-hop relationships and thus misses this vital clue leaving it with insufficient information to be confident of the match. In the Ely text snippet in Fig. 1 all three personas with Ezra Stiles Ely in their name shallow match, but the constraint insisting that a father and his son not be the same person rejects Rev. Ben Ezra Stiles Ely as being part of the

---

[1] In [8], 880 personas of 9,279 were determined to have matches. From this training set, weights were estimated (e.g. 4.6_{0908} for Birth Year, 4.8_{9474} for Father's Surname, 0.0_{0176} for Birth Town). Lawson et al. argue that these weights should be universal, depending only on the chosen set of attributes. The technique for computing the weights is described by White [14].

equivalence class of the Ezra Stiles Ely personas. Resolving the references in Fig. 4 boosts the match confidence of Hans in household B024 and Hans Böse in household B025 because the marriage dates and spouse names of the two persona records match identically.

Inter-Generational Family Tree Generation. OntoLink's process for establishing persona matches guarantees that persona records in a deep-match equivalence class can be merged. Merged personas contain all the information needed to display an inter-generational family tree as a pedigree chart, a German *Ahnentafel*, a Chinese *Jiapu*, or any other desired rendering of a family tree.

3 Field Experiments

We conducted field experiments on four books: Ely [13], Kilbarchan [7], Miller [9], and Flögeln [6]. For each, we ran the full automation pipeline from GreenQQ extraction through deep-match equivalence-class construction.

Table 1 gives statistics for generating shallow-match equivalence classes. As Sect. 2.4 explains, a shallow persona record match loosely compares names and extracted/estimated birth dates. Table 1 shows that OntoLink's curation inferred birth surnames for 31.44% of the persona records and inferred married surnames for 26.21%. For persona record birth dates, 34.15% were extracted while 58.44% were estimated with the rest being unknown. Shallow match blocking processed 34,553 persona records and generated 26,063 shallow equivalence classes.

Table 1. Persona record shallow match equivalence classes.

Book (pages)	# persona records	Surnames inf.		Birth dates		# equiv. cls. by size		
		Birth	Married	Extracted	Estimated	1	2–9	10⁺
Ely (432–700)	8,976	2,731	3,038	4,427	3,895	5,415	1,208	8
Miller (7–395)	11,439	1,532	2,573	2,818	8,303	7,749	1,554	1
Kilbarchan (4–127)	8,814	4,043	2,064	1,103	6,224	5,049	1,174	15
Flögeln (11–121)	5,324	2,557	1,382	3,451	1,771	2,924	965	1

Table 2 gives the statistics for deep matching. From the original 34,553 persona records, OntoLink generated 31,119 deep equivalence classes. The time savings by doing shallow-match blocking, which is $O(n)$, before forming deep-match equivalence classes, which is $O(n^2)$, is significant. We estimate that it would have taken more than 5 days to process *Ely* (pages 432–700) without shallow-match blocking, whereas, in actuality, it took just over 145 s. While forming these deep-match equivalence classes, OntoLink red-flagged 588 individual personas as being not self-consistent and pushed 37,287 downstream (some multiple times). Of those pushed downstream, 14,217 were unmergable, 857 were red flagged when merged (not self-consistent), and 22,213 were unconfident (lacking sufficient evidence to confidently merge). Since every red-flag error is based on an

Table 2. Persona record deep match equivalence classes.

Book (pages)	# equiv. cls. by size			# redflgd	# pushed downstream		
	1	2–9	10⁺		Unmrgbl	Merge redflgd	Not confident
Ely (432–700)	6,479	865	2	146	3,312	1	3,615
Miller (7–395)	10,164	572	41	0	2,092	5	6,493
Kilbarchan (4–127)	8,334	12	0	438	7,819	0	10,955
Flögeln (11–121)	4,084	566	0	4	994	851	1,150

Table 3. Persona deep match equivalence class accuracy.

	False positives	False negatives	# checked (Accuracy)	Accuracy*		
				Recall	Precision	F-score
Ely (432–700)	2	16	80	83%	98%	90%
Miller (7–395)	9	4	80	95%	89%	92%
Kilbarchan (4–127)	12	0	8346	100%	99.86%	99.93%
Flögeln (11–121)	1	6	80 | 732	94% | 99.3%	99% | 99.9%	96% | 99.6%

*$\textbf{Recall} = tp/(tp + fn)$, $\textbf{Precision} = tp/(tp + fp)$, where tp is true positives, fp is false positives, and fn is false negatives, and **F-score** is the harmonic mean of precision and recall, computed as $2 \cdot \frac{\text{precision} \cdot \text{recall}}{\text{precision} + \text{recall}}$.

ontologically specified constraint, a list of red-flag violations constitutes an explanation about why two persona records cannot be merged. When the evidence for a merge is deemed insufficient, a research plan for resolving the merge question can be generated. Yellow/green-flag probabilities associated with pragmatic constraints and cultural normatives and relative attribute weights indicating the importance of each kind of missing information can guide the research plan.

For Ely and Miller, we estimated the percent of false positives (erroneous deep-match equivalence classes) by checking a sampling of them. For a book's n ordered deep-match equivalence classes with two or more personas, we selected every $\lfloor n/40 \rfloor^{\text{th}}$ starting with the mth—a randomly chosen number in the range 1–40. If any one of the members of an equivalence did not match all others, the equivalence class was deemed to be a false positive. For Kilbarchan, only 12 equivalence classes with two or more personas were generated, which we checked exhaustively. Table 3 shows the resulting number of false positives.

Obtaining the percentage of false negatives (equivalence classes with missing personas) requires a ground truth that is often unreasonably difficult to obtain. However, the Ely book is organized as an inter-generational family tree and as such comprises its ground truth, and Miller lists persons alphabetically by surname helping us to know where to look for potential matching persona records. Using the same 40 Ely and Miller equivalence classes selected for checking for false positives plus the first 40 singleton equivalence classes from the ordered list of deep-match equivalence classes, we obtained the results in Table 3, including the Ely and Miller accuracy results. Having previously determined for the Kilbarchan book that no persona records match with sufficient certainty, OntoLink should return every deep equivalence class as a singleton. As Table 2 shows,

OntoLink returned 8334 singletons and 12 non-singletons (all false positives), which yields the Kilbarchan accuracy results in Table 3.

For Flögeln, we created a complete extraction ground-truth and tuned templates in an attempt to attain an F-score of 100%; but due to a few author errors and inconsistencies and a failure of GreenQQ in some line-wrap instances, we could only reach 99.9% precision and 99.8% recall for an F-score of 99.8%. Where possible, we corrected the errors and then also corrected names that, although properly extracted, contained illegal characters (e.g., slashes in the sequence "Ütjen/Itken/Itjen" as seen in Fig. 4)-about 100 corrections in total. We then curated the information in these persona records as explained in Sect. 2.3 yielding 5,976 persona records. Note that this number exceeds the number of persona records in Table 1 by 652. As explained earlier, the Flgeln book contains references (e.g., "B025" in Fig. 4), which we replace in our pipeline by the name of the referenced person. Then, before merging persona records as described in Sect. 2.4, we are able to merge persona records that contain a person name located at the same character offset on a page—a guaranteed correct record merge. Table 3 reports the accuracy with and without considering these pre-merged persona records. (The percentage of false positives and false negatives for Flögeln were estimated in the same way we estimated them for Ely and Miller.)

Correctness depends on (1) the source documents being error free (having no author-understanding or -recording mistakes, no typing/type-setting mistakes, and no OCR errors) and (2) OntoLink properly capturing and curating document-provided information. For Ely, Miller, and Kilbarchan, in checking a random sample of three pages from each book with a total of 1,022 persona record fields, precision, recall, and F-score for Linguistic Grounding with GreenQQ were respectively 90%, 81% and 86%; and for Pragmatic Constraint identification and rectification were 97%, 87%, and 92%. Checking ten randomly selected persona records from each book with a total of 453 persona record fields that were standardized, inferred, and canonicalized according to Cultural Normatives, the scores were 98%, 98%, and 98%. Observe that the F-scores increase as garnered information is curated along the OntoLink pipeline, indicating the value of ontological semantic enrichment.

The accuracy results for Flögeln reported above are measured with respect to an extraction ground truth that was meticulously prepared manually. This type of effort does not scale sufficiently to accommodate the large number of family history books that exist and have been scanned to digital format. To check performance and robustness of the OntoLink pipeline in more typical circumstances and to better understand the value of various steps in the pipeline, we performed another pair of experiments to gather more empirical evidence. We randomly selected one page in Flögeln (page 15) and primed GreenQQ by marking up only the example text found on that page. Then we ran the pipeline under four different scenarios: (1) using the Adobe Acrobat OCR engine, (2) using the ABBYY FineReader OCR engine, (3) condition 2 plus introducing page cleaning and OCR corrections, and (4) condition 3 plus allowing GreenQQ to give active feedback to the human operator to prompt for tuning details.

We measured precision, recall, and F-score across these four scenarios and then repeated the experiment with another randomly selected seed page, 46. Table 4 shows the results.

Table 4. GreenQQ extraction accuracy for Flögeln under various conditions.

	Page 15			Page 46		
	Precision	Recall	F-score	Precision	Recall	F-score
No page cleaning; no OCR corrections; Adobe Acrobat OCR engine	62%	50%	56%	62%	51%	56%
No page cleaning; no OCR corrections; ABBYY FineReader 15 OCR engine	88%	79%	83%	88%	79%	83%
With page cleaning and OCR corrections; no active learning	97%	89%	93%	97%	89%	93%
With page cleaning and OCR corrections; with active learning	98%	93%	95%	97%	93%	95%

Because the scores in Table 4 are similar for both pages 15 and 46, we can infer that the pipeline up through extraction is reasonably robust with respect to the starting point for training GreenQQ. It is also clear that the OCR engine can make a big difference (with F-scores jumping from 56% to 83% by using a more accurate OCR engine). The process of page cleaning (including training the OCR engine to ignore scanning artifacts around the edges of scanned pages and straightening skewed text lines) and correcting OCR errors also makes a difference, with F-scores improving to 93%. Finally, including "active learning" in the pipeline brings the F-scores to 95%. By *active learning* we mean that GreenQQ can identify conditions where it knows it has failed to properly extract a record. For example, if two birth are extracted for a person, GreenQQ highlights the text between the birth dates and indicates that it expected to find a person name within the highlighted text. In Fig. 4, GreenQQ extracted two birth dates, "ca. 1644" and "ca. 1637", for Casten Böse, and, indeed, a person name, "An N.N.", appears between the two dates. Note that An N.N. is not a common name form and thus is likely to be missed by common GreenQQ name templates. In fact, it is not even a name—it is a given name followed by an abbreviation of the Latin *nomen nescio* ("I do not know the name"). To resolve the problem, a GreenQQ template can be created to extract the spouse name as simply "An".

Thus, whereas creating a ground truth is quite hard, performance of the extraction pipeline can be quite good even with a much less intensive process that involves page cleaning, OCR correction, markup of one page of example templates, and then some iterative feedback to prompt for additional example templates to resolve obviously incorrect extractions.

4 Concluding Remarks

Deep-match equivalence class F-scores for [6,7,9,13] ranged from 90% to 99%. Since a collection of all deep-match equivalence classes for a book comprises its family trees, OntoLink was able to automatically create inter-generational family trees for these books with an accuracy in the 90th percentile.

Much remains to be done, such as adding location information, obtaining weights for our application data and determining whether these weights are indeed universal, improving pipeline processing, and testing more to adjust the set of constraints and fine-tune parameters and thresholds. Yet results of this preliminary study are promising. Moreover, they support the claim that enriching an ontology with linguistic grounding, pragmatic constraints, cultural normatives, and evidential reasoning can measurably enhance the work of record linkage as a contribution to digital humanities.

Acknowledgments. We thank Emeritus Professor George Nagy, Rensselaer Polytechnic Institute, for the development of GreenQQ and gratefully acknowledge the work of Gary James (Jim) Norris, who created a complete extraction ground truth for Flögeln and developed GreenQQ templates to attain near 100% extraction accuracy.

References

1. Abramitzky, R., Mill, R., Perez, S.: Linking individuals across historical sources: a fully automated approach (2018). Working Paper No. 1031
2. Bailey, M.J., Cole, C., Henderson, M., Massey, C.: How well do automated linking methods perform? Lessons from us historical data. J. Econ. Lit. **58**(4), 997–1044 (2020). https://doi.org/10.1257/jel.20191526. https://www.aeaweb.org/articles?id=10.1257/jel.20191526
3. Embley, D., Liddle, S., Park, J.: Increasing the quality of extracted information by reading between the lines. In: Comyn-Wattiau, I., du Mouza, C., Prat, N. (eds.) Ingénierie et management des systèmes d'information–Mélanges en l'honneur de Jacky Akoka. Éditions Cépaduès, Toulouse (2016)
4. Embley, D., Nagy, G.: Green interaction for extracting family information from OCR'd books. In: Proceedings of the 13th IAPR International Workshop on Document Analysis Systems, DAS 2018, pp. 127–132. IEEE Computer Society, Vienna, March 2018
5. Feigenbaum, J.: A machine learning approach to census record linking (2016). http://scholar.harvard.edu/files/jfeigenbaum/files/feigenbaumcensuslink
6. Friedrichs, E., Pech, A.: Familienbuch des Kirchspiels Flögeln: bestehend aus den Dörfern Flögeln und Fickmühlen; vom Beginn der Kirchenbücher 1700 bis 1900. Deutsche Ortssippenbücher. Reihe A, E. Friedrichs, Bremerhaven (2000)
7. Grant, F.: Index to The Register of Marriages and Baptisms in the Parish of Kilbarchan, 1649–1772. J. Skinner & Company LTD., Edinburgh (1912)

8. Lawson, J., White, D., Price, B., Yamagata, R.: Probabilistic record linkage for genealogical research. Brigham Young Univ. Stud. **41**(2), 161–174 (2002)
9. Miller Funeral Home Records, 1917–1950, Greenville, Ohio. Darke County Ohio Genealogical Society, Greenville, Ohio (1990)
10. Nagy, G.: Green information extraction from family books. SN Comput. Sci. **1**(23), 1–23 (2019). https://doi.org/10.1007/s42979-019-0024-x
11. Newcombe, H., Kennedy, J., Axford, S., James, A.: Automatic linkage of vital records. Science **130**, 954–959 (1959)
12. Packer, T.L., Embley, D.W.: Cost effective ontology population with data from lists in OCRed historical documents. In: Frinken, V., Barrett, B., Manmatha, R., Märgner, V. (eds.) HIP2013 Proceedings, pp. 44–52. ACM (2013)
13. Vanderpoel, G.: The Ely Ancestry: Lineage of RICHARD ELY of Plymouth, England. The Calumet Press, New York (1902)
14. White, D.: A review of the statistics of record linkage for genealogical research. In: Record Linkage Techniques–1997: Proceedings of an International Workshop and Exposition, pp. 362–373. National Academy Press, Washington DC, USA (1999)
15. Wilkinson, M.D., Dumontier, M., et al.: The fair guiding principles for scientific data management and stewardship. Sci. Data **3**, 1–9 (2016)
16. Woodfield, S.N., Seeger, S., Litster, S., Liddle, S.W., Grace, B., Embley, D.W.: Ontological deep data cleaning. In: Trujillo, J.C., et al. (eds.) ER 2018. LNCS, vol. 11157, pp. 100–108. Springer, Cham (2018). https://doi.org/10.1007/978-3-030-00847-5_9

Towards AI Assisted Domain Modeling

Christophe Feltus[1], Qin Ma[2], Henderik A. Proper[1,2(✉)], and Pierre Kelsen[2]

[1] Luxembourg Institute of Science and Technology, Esch-sur-Alzette, Luxembourg
christophe.feltus@list.lu, e.proper@acm.org
[2] University of Luxembourg, Esch-sur-Alzette, Luxembourg
{qin.ma,pierre.kelsen}@uni.lu

Abstract. A domain model provides an explicit knowledge representation of (selected aspects of) some domain of interest. The transition to the digital age results in an increased need for domain models that are machine understandable. We posit that, at the same time, there is an increasing need for non-experts (in modeling) to be able to create such models, or at least be able to understand the created models, and take *ownership* of their meaning and implications. This situation causes a 'modeling bottleneck' in that it is not reasonable to expect all non-experts to become modeling experts. This is where we turn to AI as an enabling technology to support non-experts in domain modeling related tasks; i.e, AI Assisted Domain Modeling. We foresee a symbiotic collaboration between human intelligence, symbolic AI and subsymbolic AI; essentially resulting in a triple-helix of human, symbolic, and subsymbolic intelligence.

The aim of this workshop paper is to structurally explore the potential role of (symbolic and subsymbolic) AI to support domain conceptualization. To do so, we will combine three perspectives on domain modeling: (1) a framework relating the different conceptions (harbored in the mind of a modeler) regarding the domain to be modeled, and the model itself, (2) the role of normative frames towards modeling activities, and (3) modeling as a structured dialogue between an (automated) system analyst and a domain expert.

1 Introduction

A domain model provides an explicit knowledge representation of (selected aspects of) some domain of interest. Such a domain of interest may e.g. involve an existing part of an enterprise, or an envisioned future situation, etc. [38,39]. Software engineering, information systems engineering, and enterprise engineering, have a rich tradition in the use of different kind of domain models. This includes a.o.: enterprise (architecture) models, business process models, organizational models, information models, software models, ontologies, knowledge graphs, etc. In line with [38,39], we consider each of these kinds of models as valued members of the larger family of *domain models*.[1]

---

[1] Not all domain models are *conceptual models*. As discussed in e.g. [38], a distinction could be made between *conceptual* domain models and *computational design* models, where the latter involve 'compromises' needed to support computational (design) considerations to e.g. support simulation, animation, or even execution of the model.

© Springer Nature Switzerland AG 2021
I. Reinhartz-Berger and S. Sadiq (Eds.): ER 2021 Workshops, LNCS 13012, pp. 75–89, 2021.
https://doi.org/10.1007/978-3-030-88358-4_7

In our present day society, we can observe a strong increase in the role/use of knowledge-intensive computing technology, including *(explainable) AI*, *data science*, and *digital twins* [29]. Meanwhile, such knowledge-intensive computing technologies have permeated virtually all facets of society. From manufacturing, logistics, finance, health, to space exploration. With this increase, also comes an increase in the need to capture relevant domain knowledge by means of domain models in a format which is understandable by both humans and 'machines'.[2]

As a result, there is an increasing need for non-experts (in modeling) to be able to create such models, or at least be able to understand the created models, and take *ownership* of their meaning and implications. The authors of [43] also observe how modeling increasingly becomes embedded in everyday work. The latter makes it inevitable for non-experts (in modeling) to also be able to engage in modeling activities. This situation causes a 'modeling bottleneck' in the sense that it is not reasonable to expect all non-experts to become modeling experts.

Moreover, supporting modeling processes is one of the major challenges for domain modeling, as observed in [36]. This challenge has fueled earlier efforts to make modeling strategies more explicit [24–26], as well as experiments with the concept of *natural modeling* [8,47], which has also been echoed by the more recent notion of *grassroots modeling* [43].

The authors of [43] suggest the use of *assistive technologies* to support modeling activities by non-experts. Inspired by this, we prefer to speak about *Assisted Domain Modeling*. Furthermore, we turn to AI as an enabling technology to drive the needed assistance, hence AI Assisted Domain Modeling. More specifically, we foresee a symbiotic collaboration between human intelligence, symbolic AI and subsymbolic AI for assisting domain modeling, which essentially results in a triple-helix of human, symbolic-driven and subsymbolic-driven intelligence.

A critical aspect in the creation and interpretation of domain models is the conceptualization of the domain that is (to be) captured in the model [39]. Therefore, we initially focus on this aspect.

In line with this, the aim of this *workshop paper*, is to work towards a structural exploration of the potential role of AI to support domain conceptualization. To do so, we will combine three existing perspectives regarding domain modeling: (**p1**) a framework [38,39] relating the different conceptions (as harbored in the mind of an modeler) regarding the domain to be modeled, and the model itself, (**p2**) the role of normative frames [36] towards modeling activities, and (**p3**) viewing modeling as a structured dialogue between an (automated) system analyst and a domain expert [9]. The integration of these perspectives will enable us to more closely investigate the potential role of AI to support domain conceptualization. In this paper, we will also take first steps towards the latter.

An important disclaimer we need to make here, is that for now, we do not (yet) consider a situation where multiple modelers collaborate in the creation of a domain, i.e., collaborative modeling.

---

[2] But this does not necessarily imply that these models should be executable.

The remainder of this paper is structured as follows. In Sect. 2 we present an integrated view on domain modeling, which combines perspectives **p1** and **p2**. In moving towards AI Assisted Domain Modeling, Sect. 3 then complements this with perspective **p3** to arrive at a framework to understand/position the key activities involved in domain modeling in general, and conceptualization in particular. Based on this, Sect. 4 provides a short reflection on the possible role of AI to support domain modeling. Section 5 and Sect. 6 then explore the potential role of symbolical and subsymbolic AI, respectively, to support/drive the involved activities. In Sect. 7 we conclude the paper, while also reflecting on next steps towards the elaboration of the presented framework, as well as concrete experiments towards AI support.

2   Understanding Domain Modeling

In line with [7,38,39], we consider a *domain model* to be: A *social artifact* that is *acknowledged* by an *observer* to *represent* an *abstraction* of some *domain* for a particular *purpose*.

A model is a *social artifact* in the sense that its role as a model should be recognizable by (a) collective agent(s) [39]. For this reason, it should exist outside of our minds. In our field of application, this artifact often takes the *form* of some 'boxes-and-lines' diagram. More generally, however, domain models can, depending on the *purpose* at hand, take other forms as well, including text, mathematical specifications, games, animations, simulations, and physical objects. It is ultimately the observer who needs to *acknowledge* the fact that an *artifact* is indeed a model of the domain, for the given *purpose*. Since a model is the representation of an *abstraction* of the domain, some 'details' of the domain are consciously left out, in line with the *purpose* of the model.

In the context of modeling, and following [39], we suggest to make a distinction between two kinds of (composed) thoughts that the observer may have about the domain: *conceptions* and *perceptions*. When actors observe a domain, they will obtain (through their senses) a *perception*. They may than be able to interpret, structure, and/or further abstract this *perception* to form a *conception* in terms of concepts and relations among the concepts.

In *perceiving*, the multitude of facets and nuances of the world around us, forces us to apply filters. When creating a conception from our perception, we tend to filter even further, consciously leaving out details in order to be able to focus on what we think is important (in particular when creating models). This is also where we apply our 'hard-wired' ability to classify our observations and make generalizations [31,32].

As a consequence of the above, a modeler (be it an expert modeler or a non-expert modeler) needs to harbor (at least) four conceptions [39] in their mind: (1) a 'full' conception of the domain (as they 'sense' it); (2) a conception of the purpose for the model; (3) a filtered focused conception of the domain, based on the purpose of the model; and (4) a conception of the artifact that is (to be) the model representing the focused domain conception. These four conceptions are

shown (as circles) within the darker gray area, labeled Foreground Conceptions, of
Fig. 1. The rectangles represent the externally (to the actor) observable Purpose,
Domain, etc. Figure 1 also shows how the (conception of the) *purpose* of the
domain model, influences/modifies the observation and focus. This structure is
based on [39], where we have now modified some of the terms to better clarify
the fact that the *domain focus* is the conception that results after the *purposeful*
filtering/abstraction of the original 'raw' conception of the domain.

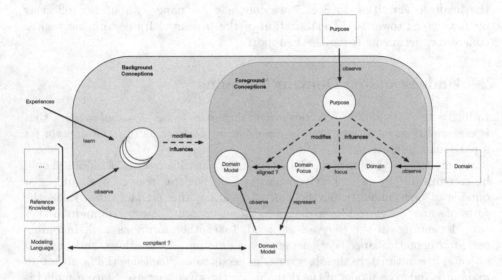

Fig. 1. Conceptions playing a role in domain modeling

One of the challenges when expressing the *domain focus* in terms of a *domain
model* is to make sure that the latter is 'shaped' in such a way that it corresponds
to the former. However, since the *domain model* is external to the modeler, this
operationally means that the conception of the *domain model* needs to be aligned
to the *domain focus* conception.

It should be noted that Fig. 1 actually captures two possible scenarios: (1) a
modeler creating a model of a domain, in line with the purpose, and (2) a (non-
expert) modeler who is asked to acknowledge a given (i.e. created by another
modeler) model as being a valid model (of the domain, in line with the purpose).

The above discussion covers perspective **p1**, concerning different conceptions involved in domain modeling. This takes us to **p2**, i.e., the role of normative frames. As argued in [36,39], modeling is influenced/modified by several *normative frames*, including the used design/engineering framework, the
(to be used) modeling language, personal biases, etc. These normative frames
influence/modify the Foreground Conceptions as shown in the dark gray area of
Fig. 1. When the modeler has an explicit understanding of the normative frames
they (consciously or unconsciously) use, this results in additional conceptions.

In Fig. 1, this is shown as the Background Conceptions pertaining to e.g., the definition of a modeling language, reference models, gained experience, etc.

3   Supporting Domain Modeling

In this Section, we look at the question of how a modeling processes can be supported, more specifically in terms of the concept of a *modeling assistant*. In doing so, we will not yet make a choice if such a *modeling assistant* should involve human intelligence or any form of AI. This question will be considered in more detail in the next Sections.

In [9,24–26], the authors take the perspective (**p3**) that a modeling process involves a structured dialogue between a *domain expert* and a *system analyst*. We contend that such a *structured dialogue*, which can also be seen as a kind of a 'think aloud protocol', provides a good vantage point to support domain modeling, in particular, when it is a (machine) observable dialogue. The ambitions, as reported in [9,24–26], also point towards strategies behind such a structured dialogue. Moreover, the perspective on a modeling process as a structured dialogue, also resulted in hypotheses on the competences required from the participants in a modeling process [15].

We will, therefore, take the *structured dialogue* perspective as a starting point in identifying ways to support modeling processes. However, since we are concerned with the challenge of providing modelers in general (be they experts in modeling or not) with more support for their modeling activities, we actually prefer not to speak about a distinction between a *domain expert* and a *system analyst*, but rather speak about a *modeler* and a *modeling assistant*.

It should also be noted that the assumptions as made in [15] regarding the roles and competencies required for a modeling process, 'silently' puts the onus of the initial *domain conceptualization* on the domain expert. For instance, it is assumed that "*domain experts can provide any number of significant sample sentences in relation to relevant information objects*". This implies, however, that the domain expert must already have a clear *domain conception* [39] in their mind. As such, we certainly acknowledge the work done in [15], while at the same time being more ambitious: *Can domain experts be supported in conceptualizing their domain of expertise?* In particular, when moving from the initial *domain conception* to the conception of a *focused domain* that is in line with the modeling *purpose* at hand.

Building on the concept of *structured (modeling) dialogues*, we propose the framework as shown in Fig. 2. At the top, we find, following Fig. 1, a modeler observes a domain, and then given a purpose, aims to produce (or validate) a domain model. At the bottom, we find a modeling assistant. For a modeling assistant to aid a modeler, 'it' should have an understanding of the foreground and background conceptions as held by the supported modeler (resulting in the P', D', DF' and DM' 'shadow' conceptions). We contend that the only way for the modeling assistant to develop this understanding, is to (1) observe the actions of the modeler and develop a Modeler profile; (2) conduct a structured dialogue

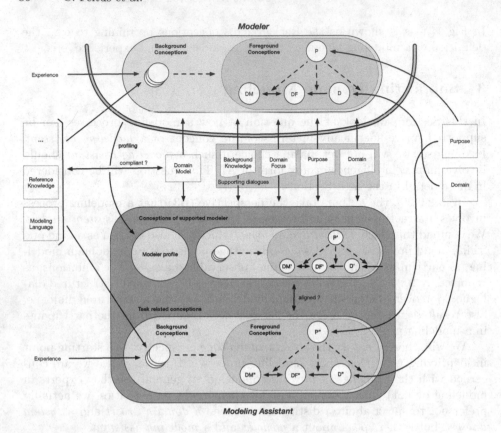

Fig. 2. Support for domain modeling

regarding the different conceptions held by the modeler (see the rectangle labeled with Supporting dialogues); and/or (3) co-create the actual Domain model. Ideally, a modeler would (be nudged to) use a 'think-aloud' strategy when modeling a domain. More specifically, making their considerations explicit (preferably in a machine understandable format), will be beneficial in driving the structured dialogue(s) needed for the modeling assistant to derive an approximation of the conceptions held by the modeler.

Since the modeling assistant is likely able to observe/read itself the modeling purpose, the domain to be modeled, the definition of the modeling language to be used (potentially even in a machine readable format), background knowledge, etc., the modeling assistant may also harbor a conception of the purpose, the domain, the domain focus, etc., in line with the modeling task at hand, resulting in the conceptions P", D", DF" and DM".

The combination of these, allows the modeling assistant to aid the modeler in their task to create a domain model and/or understand/validate/evaluate an existing domain model in relation to its purpose and the domain.

4 Towards AI Support

When using AI as an enabling technology to realize modeling assistants, the conceptions as (to be) harbored in 'the mind' of the AI assistants will take the form of trained statistical networks and/or more traditional machine understandable representations. In [12], the author provides a (not exhaustive) categorization of modeling related 'problems' that may be supported by means of AI. Using these categories as a base, combined with Fig. 2, this would give rise to the following first identification of potential AI support.

Gathering Background Knowledge

- **Pattern mining in models:** Reusable similar modeling components are identified by mining typical modeling patterns [19].
- **Finding matches between modeling constructs:** Identification of similar modeling constructs in different models [3].

Supporting Structured Modeling Dialogues

- **Modeling guidance:** Syntactic, semantic, or pragmatic guidance is provided during the step-by-step refinement/specialization of the models by the modeler [1,2,6,10,35,37,40,42].
- **Explicit strategies for modeling** [23,26].

Correction and Validation of Models

- **Automatic modeling and model correction:** Models are automatically corrected, or developed by automated planning [21].

Model Representation and Interpretation

- **Model-to-Text, Text-to-Model or Picture-to-Model:** Natural texts, dialogues, and pictures are transformed into models and vice versa [17,22, 23,41,46].

In the next two Sections, we discuss the potential AI contributions related to these categories in more detail.

5 A Potential Role for Symbolic AI

Symbolic AI methods represent knowledge using a symbol-based representation [13]. For instance, in the form of graphs, logic formulas, symbolic rules, and relies on formal operations, such as inference and production, over the symbolic representation of knowledge to simulate mental or cognitive operations.

In [20], John Haugeland coined the term GOFAI ("Good Old-Fashioned Artificial Intelligence"). One may argue that (good old) symbolic AI is 'old-fashioned', especially when compared to the present advances in 'data- and statistics-driven' subsymbolic AI techniques. However, there is still consider-able value in symbolic AI. For example, it is good for addressing problems that need logical inference on knowledge representation. Symbolic AI techniques, such as problem solving in terms of constraints satisfaction, Natural Language pro-cessing (NLP), and logical inference, are still among the core functionalities of current AI systems. Moreover, symbolic AI can provide good solution in circum-stances where statistical approaches fall short, e.g., when there is not enough data available. Symbolic reasoning also provides inherently more transparency regarding the reasoning process, thus enabling explainable AI more easily.

In fact, many researchers start to resort to the combination of both kinds of AI when designing a solution for their problems. For example, [42] exploits both rule-based NLP techniques and data-driven ML techniques to design a web-based bot that can automatically extract domain models (class diagrams) from domain problem descriptions, and demonstrates that the combined solution out-performs others where only one style of AI techniques is applied.

Let us come back to the process of assisted domain conceptualization as depicted Fig. 2 and point out some example steps for which symbolic AI can pro-vide help. The process starts with both modeler and modeling assistant observing the domain to be modeled, the purpose of modeling, any contextual normative frames, and forming a conception of each. This step involves the three generic mental operations (acts) coined by St. Thomas Acquinas [16]: defining concepts, pronouncing judgments (relations) between concepts, and reasoning new knowl-edge from knowledge existing in a knowledge base constructed by the first two acts. We acknowledge that the domain, the purpose, and the normative frames can exist in various formats, e.g., as a physical object, a document in natural language, a vocal agreement, or a picture. Depending on the format and the sensing channels used by the modeler and the modeling assistant during the observation, various rule-based AI techniques such as NLP (Natural Language Processing), and pattern recognition, can be exploited.

When both modeler and assistant form the individual conceptions, they com-municate (through dialogues or Q&A sessions) with each other to understand counterpart's conceptions, to validate, to update, to improve, and eventually to agree upon on an aligned conceptualization of the referents, uttered in the form of artifacts. In this aspect, if the assistant is a computer, conversational AI techniques, such as dialogue systems, conversational agents, and chat-bots, will be the areas to resort to. Such systems can e.g. be used to operationalize the rule-based modeling strategies as suggested in e.g. [9,18,24,27,30].

Moreover, existing symbolic AI approaches, such as recommender systems can be leveraged to provide guidance for structured modeling dialogues. As an example, the work of Agt-Rickauer et al. [1,2] demonstrates how symbolic AI techniques can be jointly exploited to support domain modeling. More specifi-cally, they use rule-based NLP techniques and knowledge representation tech-niques to access domain knowledge from heterogeneous sources, including tex-tual data sets and existing knowledge bases (such as ontologies), and make use of a recommender system to offer semantic (vs. syntactical) modeling support/recommendation to modelers in various modeling scenarios, by capitalizing on the domain knowledge gathered in the first part.

6 A Potential Role for Subsymbolic AI

In this Section, we review some *subsymbolic* AI approaches that can potentially be used in the context of a modeling assistant.

Principal Component Analysis (PCA) is a well-known ML technique [28] that aims to reduce the number of dimensions of large data without losing too much information. This age-old technique is now embedded in ML libraries[3] and now benefits of more computational power than ever. It is based on the fact that many types of vector spatial data are compressible, and compression can be performed more efficiently by sampling. The main advantages of PCA are better data visualization and optimization of resources when the PCA is used to prepare the data before processing by another algorithm.

There is little scientific contribution which exploits PCA for modeling purposes. Nevertheless, [10] illustrates the use of PCA for *modeling assistance* (towards *model representation & interpretation*) by investigating the effect of structural complexity on the understandability of state-chart diagrams. The authors identified three types of complexity, namely: (1) the size and control flow complexity of the state-chart, (2) the actions performed when entering or leaving a state, and (3) the sequence of actions performed within the state. Based on this, elaborated a prediction model to understand the impact of the complexities on the state-chart understandably. To identify the components of structural complexity, [10] uses the Principal Component Analysis statistical data reduction method.

Clustering Algorithms[4] aim to gather types of machine learning unsupervised algorithms that group various (unlabelled) objects into clusters based on the object's features.

Consider, for instance, a database of activities (unlabelled objects) described by a set of features like the *activities' inputs and outputs, the stakeholders involved in the activity, the activity duration, or the previous and next activities*, etc. This database may be represented as an input matrix for a clustering algorithm and the output vector of that algorithm is a set of n clusters of activities like, e.g., *send a message, validate a reply, make an order*, etc. These clusters may consist in a relevant information to support the conceptualization of generic activities to be used afterwards to elaborate, for example, a process model.

Some famous clustering algorithms are K-Means, Mean-Shift, Agglomerative Clustering, DBScan, etc. In that list, K-Means [33] aims to split the observed data into K clusters in which each observation is included in the cluster with

---

[3] https://scikit-learn.org/stable/modules/generated/sklearn.decomposition.PCA.html.

[4] https://scikit-learn.org/stable/modules/clustering.html.

the nearest mean. K-Means consists by the way to minimize the within-cluster sum-of-squares value.

Clustering naturally contributes to the modeling tasks of *pattern mining in models* and *finding matches between modeling constructs*. Additionally, clustering may also contribute to other tasks such as the *automatic modeling and model correction*. For instance, [6] exploits clustering algorithms for *automatic refactoring* of UML diagrams. Therefore, the authors address the software refactoring at the design time and at the UML diagram level. At the software-side, refactoring means *changing the internal structure of a software to make it easier to understand and cheaper to modify without changing its observable behavior* [14]. In [19], clustering is used to support *pattern mining in models*. The authors exploit the RPST (Refined Process Structure Tree) to derive trees of nested process fragments from different models. Patterns are afterward determined among these nested fragments.

Classification Algorithms[5] involves supervised algorithms that, when trained, can classify objects based on their features. A classical example is the classification of the Iris flower. A machine learning model is trained with a dataset containing three types of labeled input corresponding to Iris species (Iris setosa, Iris virginica and Iris versicolor) and described by four features: length and width of sepals and petals. When trained, the model allows identifying new samples based on its features only.

Transposed to the modeling task of e.g. *finding matches between modeling constructs*, a machine learning model can be trained to, for instance, improve the classification of business activities into three types of ArchiMate [5] elements (*business process, business function* and *business task*) based on features such as *the duration of the activity, the level of description of this activity, the number of stakeholders involved*, etc. When a new activity must be conceptualized, the trained machine learning model can then help in classifying it in *business process, business function* or *business task*.

Convolutional Neural Networks (CNNs) [4] are used for image classification (e.g., detect objects in picture). The input of a CNN is very often an image (but it may be any type of data object) represented by an array of pixels, and the output is the class to which the image has a probability of belonging. Such algorithms are made up two parts. The first part consists of a feature extractor and the second part consists of a set of fully connected layers which takes the feature vectors as input and maps them to a final layer where each neuron corresponds to the predicted class (e.g., a dog, a cat, a circle, a square, etc.).

CNNs can play a role with regards to *Picture-to-Model* tasks. For instance, in the recent paper [17], the authors propose a CNN based tool to classify an input images as UML class diagrams and non-UML class diagrams or in [46], the authors propose a application to recognize the structure of business process models drawn on paper and whiteboard. Thereby, AI is exploited to create digital versions of the models. Yet another interesting contributions is the

---

[5] https://scikit-learn.org/stable/supervised_learning.html.

classification of class diagrams that has been investigated by means of image classification in [22]. After applying image classification to class diagrams, the features extracted were tested with five machine learners to assess the accuracy of their classification.

Recurrent Neural Networks (RNNs) [44] are often used for speech recognition. At times, the domain to be modeled may also have been described (partially) by speech. E.g., a process owner describing a process during an interview. This oral description needs first to be transcribed into a text.

In those cases, the analysis output of the first piece of data (e.g. a word) needs to be considered for the analysis of the subsequent ones. The output of an RNN can be analyzed further by other algorithms in order to extract the important elements that it contains such as, for the description of a process: *the tasks, the stakeholders, the inputs* or *outputs*, etc. To do this, other techniques may be used such as the word embedding which is a *language modeling tool* that consists in learning the representation of words from a text based on their semantics, on the context, and/or on their occurrences in a text.

Word embedding, together with the transformer mechanism, is already used for sentiment analysis, question answering, and text-summarization tasks. It could also be extended for domain conceptualization.

In the field of text-to-model mining, on overview of the current state of the art is provided in [41]. The paper presents different approaches focusing on business process models. These approaches are analyzed and compared against each other both at a theoretical and a technical point of view.

Reinforcement Learning (RL) involves software agents learning to react on their own to an environment that they do not yet know [45]. In order to learn how to react, agents make decisions and take actions with the objective of accumulating rewards while avoiding errors.

Despite RLs' exponential deployment [11], as far as our knowledge, there is not yet a sound scientific contribution that addresses the conceptualization with reinforcement learning, we believe that the discovery of new concept considering this AI technique makes perfect sense. Indeed, the activity of conceptualization is a gradual activity, during which the modeler learns to discover new concepts by improving his reasoning from his successes and his mistakes.

This learning method is therefore naturally assimilated to the learning algorithms offered by reinforcement learning which also consists of discovering information with back and forth steps, and trial and error. It would therefore not be surprising that further research develops within a few years in this area and contributes to the activities of *pattern mining in models* and/or *finding matches between modeling constructs*.

7   Conclusion

The aim of this workshop paper, was to work towards a structural exploration of the potential role of (symbolic and subsymbolic) AI to support domain conceptualization. In doing so, we first combined three existing perspectives on domain modeling: (1) a framework relating the different conceptions (harbored in the mind of a modeler) regarding the domain to be modeled, and the model itself, (2) the role of normative frames towards modeling activities, and (3) modeling as a structured dialogue between an (automated) system analyst and a domain expert. This resulted in a general understanding of the (conceptualization) activities involved in domain modeling (Fig. 1), as well as a first understanding of the core functionalities that would be needed from a *modeling assistant* (Fig. 2). In terms of this, we then provided an initial survey of the potential role of symbolic and subsymbolic AI in supporting domain modeling, where we foresee a symbiotic collaboration between human intelligence, symbolic AI and subsymbolic AI.

As the next step, we aim to (1) further elaborate our understanding of the potential role of modeling assistance (i.e. elaborate on Fig. 2, while also including a collaborative modeling perspective), (2) elaborate the survey of available AI approaches and techniques that may be used to provide modeling assistance, and (3) initiate a series of experiments with different strategies/techniques for modeling support.

References

1. Agt-Rickauer, H.: Supporting domain modeling with automated knowledge acquisition and modeling recommendations. Ph.D. thesis, Technical University of Berlin, Germany (2020)
2. Agt-Rickauer, H., Kutsche, R.D., Sack, H.: Domore - a recommender system for domain modeling. In: Proceedings of the 6th International Conference on Model-Driven Engineering and Software Development, MODELSWARD 2018, Funchal, Madeira - Portugal, 22–24 January 2018, pp. 71–82. SciTePress (2018)
3. Ahmed, J., Huang, M.: Classification of role stereotypes for classes in UML class diagrams using machine learning (2020). https://gupea.ub.gu.se/handle/2077/67955
4. Albawi, S., Mohammed, T.A., Al-Zawi, S.: Understanding of a convolutional neural network. In: 2017 International Conference on Engineering and Technology (ICET), pp. 1–6 (2017)
5. Band, I., et al.: ArchiMate 3.0 specification. The Open Group (2016)
6. Baqais, A., Alshayeb, M.: Automatic refactoring of single and multiple-view UML models using artificial intelligence algorithms. In: Doctoral Consortium (MODELSWARD 2016), pp. 3–8. INSTICC, SciTePress (2016)
7. Bjeković, M., Proper, H.A., Sottet, J.-S.: Embracing pragmatics. In: Yu, E., Dobbie, G., Jarke, M., Purao, S. (eds.) ER 2014. LNCS, vol. 8824, pp. 431–444. Springer, Cham (2014). https://doi.org/10.1007/978-3-319-12206-9_37
8. Bjeković, M., Sottet, J.S., Favre, J.M., Proper, H.A.: A framework for natural enterprise modelling. In: IEEE 15th Conference on Business Informatics, CBI 2013, Vienna, Austria, 15–18 July 2013, pp. 79–84. IEEE Computer Society Press (2013)
9. van Bommel, P., Hoppenbrouwers, S.J.B.A., Proper, H.A., van der Weide, T.P.: Exploring modelling strategies in a meta-modelling context. In: Meersman et al. [34], pp. 1128–1137
10. Cruz-Lemus, J.A., et al.: The impact of structural complexity on the understandability of UML statechart diagrams. Inf. Sci. **180**(11), 2209–2220 (2010)

11. Feltus, C.: A I's contribution to ubiquitous systems and pervasive networks security- reinforcement learning vs. recurrent Networks. J. Ubiquit. Syst. Pervasive Netw. **15**(02), 1–9 (2021)
12. Fettke, P.: Conceptual modelling and artificial intelligence: overview and research challenges from the perspective of predictive business process management. In: Companion Proceedings of Modellierung 2020 Short, Workshop and Tools & Demo Papers co-located with Modellierung 2020, Vienna, Austria, 19–21 February 2020. CEUR Workshop Proceedings, vol. 2542, pp. 157–164 (2020)
13. Flasiński, M.: Introduction to Artificial Intelligence. Springer, Heidelberg (2016)
14. Fowler, M.: Refactoring: Improving the Design of Existing Code. Addison-Wesley Professional (2018)
15. Frederiks, P.J.M., van der Weide, T.P.: Information modeling: the process and the required competencies of its participants. Data Knowl. Eng. **58**(1), 4–20 (2006)
16. Gilby, T.: St. Thomas Aquinas Philosophical Texts. Oxford University Press, Oxford (1951)
17. Gosala, B., et al.: Automatic classification of UML class diagrams using deep learning technique: convolutional neural network. Appl. Sci. **11**(9), 4267 (2021)
18. Guizzardi, G., Prince Sale, T.: "As simple as possible but not simpler": towards an ontology model canvas. In: Borgo, S., Kutz, O., Loebe, F., Neuhaus, F. (eds.) Proceedings of the Joint Ontology Workshops 2017 - Episode 3: The Tyrolean Autumn of Ontology, Bozen-Bolzano, Italy (2017)
19. Hake, P., Fettke, P., Loos, P.: Automatic pattern mining in repositories of graph-based process models. In: Multikonferenz Wirtschaftsinf, pp. 1143–1154 (2016)
20. Haugeland, J.: Artificial Intelligence: The Very Idea. Massachusetts Institute of Technology, USA (1985)
21. Heinrich, B., Klier, M., Zimmermann, S.: Automated planning of process models: design of a novel approach to construct exclusive choices. Decis. Support Syst. **78**, 1–14 (2015)
22. Hjaltason, J., Samúelsson, I.: Automatic classification of UML Class diagrams through image feature extraction and machine learning (2015)
23. Hoppenbrouwers, S., Wilmont, I.: Focused conceptualisation: framing questioning and answering in model-oriented dialogue games. In: van Bommel, P., Hoppenbrouwers, S., Overbeek, S., Proper, E., Barjis, J. (eds.) PoEM 2010. LNBIP, vol. 68, pp. 190–204. Springer, Heidelberg (2010). https://doi.org/10.1007/978-3-642-16782-9_14
24. Hoppenbrouwers, S.J.B.A., Lindeman, L., Proper, H.A.: Capturing modeling processes - towards the modial modeling laboratory. In: Meersman et al. [34], pp. 1242–1252
25. Hoppenbrouwers, S.J.B.A., Proper, H.A.E., van der Weide, T.P.: A fundamental view on the process of conceptual modeling. In: Delcambre, L., Kop, C., Mayr, H.C., Mylopoulos, J., Pastor, O. (eds.) ER 2005. LNCS, vol. 3716, pp. 128–143. Springer, Heidelberg (2005). https://doi.org/10.1007/11568322_9
26. Hoppenbrouwers, S.J.B.A., Proper, H.A., Weide, T.P.v.d.: Towards explicit strategies for modeling. In: Halpin, T.A., Siau, K., Krogstie, J. (eds.) Proceedings of the 10th Workshop on Evaluating Modeling Methods for Systems Analysis and Design (EMMSAD 2005), Held in Conjunction with the 17th Conference on Advanced Information Systems (CAiSE 2005), pp. 485–492 (2005)
27. Hoppenbrouwers, S.J.B.A., Rouwette, E.A.J.A.: A dialogue game for analysing group model building: framing collaborative modelling and its facilitation. Int. J. Organ. Design Eng. (IJODE) **2**(1), 19–40 (2012)

28. Hotelling, H.: Analysis of a complex of statistical variables into principal components. J. Educ. Psychol. **24**(6), 417 (1933)
29. Jones, D., Snider, S., Nassehi, A., Yon, J., Hicks, B.: Characterizing the digital twin: a systematic literature review. CIRP J. Manuf. Sci. Technol. **29**, 36–52 (2020)
30. Kelsen, P., Ma, Q., Glodt, C.: A lightweight modeling approach based on functional decomposition. J. Object Technol. **19**(2), 15:1–22 (2020). The 16th European Conference on Modelling Foundations and Applications (ECMFA 2020)
31. Lakoff, G.: Women, Fire, and Dangerous Things: What Categories Reveal About the Mind. University of Chicago Press, Chicago (1997)
32. Lakoff, G., Johnson, M.: Metaphors We Live By. University of Chicago Press, Chicago (2003)
33. Lloyd, S.: Least squares quantization in PCM. IEEE Trans. Inf. Theory **28**(2), 129–137 (1982)
34. Meersman, R., Tari, Z., Herrero, P. (eds.): On the Move to Meaningful Internet Systems 2006: OTM 2006 Workshops, OTM Confederated International Workshops and Posters, AWeSOMe, CAMS, COMINF, IS, KSinBIT, MIOS-CIAO, MONET, OnToContent, ORM, PerSys, OTM Academy Doctoral Consortium, RDDS, SWWS, and SeBGIS 2006, Montpellier, France, 29 October–3 November 2006. Proceedings, Part II. LNCS, vol. 4278. Springer, Heidelberg (2006)
35. Mussbacher, G., et al.: Opportunities in intelligent modeling assistance. Softw. Syst. Model. **19**(5), 1045–1053 (2020). https://doi.org/10.1007/s10270-020-00814-5
36. Proper, H.A., Bjeković, M.: Fundamental challenges in systems modelling. EMISA Forum **39**(1), 13–28 (2019)
37. Proper, H.A., Bjeković, M., van Gils, B., Hoppenbrouwers, S.J.B.A.: Towards a multi-stage strategy to teach enterprise modelling. In: Aveiro, D., Guizzardi, G., Guerreiro, S., Guédria, W. (eds.) EEWC 2018. LNBIP, vol. 334, pp. 181–202. Springer, Cham (2019). https://doi.org/10.1007/978-3-030-06097-8_12
38. Proper, H.A., Guizzardi, G.: On domain modelling and requisite variety. In: Grabis, J., Bork, D. (eds.) PoEM 2020. LNBIP, vol. 400, pp. 186–196. Springer, Cham (2020). https://doi.org/10.1007/978-3-030-63479-7_13
39. Proper, H.A., Guizzardi, G.: On domain conceptualization. In: Aveiro, D., Guizzardi, G., Pergl, R., Proper, H.A. (eds.) EEWC 2020. LNBIP, vol. 411, pp. 49–69. Springer, Cham (2021). https://doi.org/10.1007/978-3-030-74196-9_4
40. Proper, H.A., Weide, T.P.v.d.: Modelling as selection of interpretation. In: Mayr, H.C., Breu, H. (eds.) Modellierung 2006, 22.-24. März 2006, Innsbruck, Tirol, Austria, Proceedings. LNI, vol. P82, pp. 223–232. Gesellschaft für Informatik, Bonn (2006). https://tinyurl.com/y3h4uas9
41. Riefer, M., Ternis, S.F., Thaler, T.: Mining process models from natural language text: a state-of-the-art analysis. Multikonferenz Wirtschaftsinformatik (MKWI-16), pp. 9–11, March 2016
42. Saini, R., Mussbacher, G., Guo, J.L.C., Kienzle, J.: DoMoBOT: a bot for automated and interactive domain modelling. In: MODELS 2020: ACM/IEEE 23rd International Conference on Model Driven Engineering Languages and Systems, Canada, 18–23 October 2020, Companion Proceedings, pp. 45:1–45:10. ACM (2020)
43. Sandkuhl, K., et al.: From expert discipline to common practice: a vision and research agenda for extending the reach of enterprise modeling. Bus. Inform. Syst. Eng. **60**(1), 69–80 (2018). https://doi.org/10.1007/s12599-017-0516-y

44. Sherstinsky, A.: Fundamentals of recurrent neural network (RNN) and long short-term memory (LSTM) network. Phys. D: Nonlinear Phenomena **404** (2020). https://doi.org/10.1016/j.physd.2019.132306
45. Van Otterlo, M., Wiering, M.: Reinforcement learning and Markov decision processes. In: Wiering, M., van Otterlo, M. (eds.) Reinforcement learning, vol. 12, pp. 3–42. Springer, Heidelberg (2012). https://doi.org/10.1007/978-3-642-27645-3_1
46. Zapp, M., Fettke, P., Loos, P.: Towards a software prototype supporting automatic recognition of sketched business process models. Wirtschaftsinformatik und Angewandte Informatik (2017)
47. Zarwin, Z., Bjeković, M., Favre, J.M., Sottet, J.S., Proper, H.A.: Natural modelling. J. Object Technol. **13**(3), 4:1–4:36 (2014)

Conceptual Modeling for Life Sciences (CMLS) 2021

CMLS 2021 Preface

The recent advances in unravelling the secrets of human conditions and diseases have encouraged new paradigms for their prevention, diagnosis, and treatment. As the information is increasing at an unprecedented rate, it directly impacts the design and future development of information and data management pipelines; thus, new ways of processing data, information, and knowledge in health care environments are strongly needed.

The International Workshop on Conceptual Modeling for Life Sciences (CMLS) was held in 2021 in its second edition. Its objective is to be both a meeting point for information systems (IS), conceptual modeling (CM), and data management (DM) researchers working on health care and life science problems, and an opportunity to share and discuss new approaches to improve promising fields, with a special focus on genomic data management – how to use the information from the genome to better understand biological and clinical features – and precision medicine – giving each patient an individualized treatment by understanding the peculiar aspects of the disease. From the precise ontological characterization of the components involved in complex biological systems to the modeling of the operational processes and decision support methods used in the diagnosis and prevention of disease, the joined research communities of IS, CM, and DM have an important role to play; they must help in providing feasible solutions for high-quality and efficient health care.

The recent COVID-19 pandemic has attracted increasing attention to the genetic mechanisms of humans and viruses. CMLS aims to become an additional forum for discussing the responsibility of the conceptual modeling community in supporting the life sciences related to this new reality.

This second edition of CMLS attracted high-quality submissions centered around the modeling of data, systems, and processes of the life sciences domain. Four papers were selected after a blind review process that involved at least two experts from the field for each submission. All of the selected papers provide significant insights related to the problem under investigation, and they contributed to an interesting technical program to stimulate discussion. We expect a growing interest in this area in the coming years; this was one of the motivations for continuing our commitment to this workshop in conjunction with the ER 2021 conference.

Acknowledgements. We would like to express our gratitude to Stefano Ceri and Oscar Pastor who demonstrated continuous support to the organization of this workshop. We also thank the Program Committee members for their hard work in reviewing papers, the authors for submitting their works, and the ER 2021 organizing committee for supporting our workshop. We also thank ER 2021 workshop chairs Shazia Sadiq and Iris Reinhartz-Berger for their direction and guidance. CMLS 2021 was organized within the framework of the following projects: ERC Advanced Grant 693174 "Data-driven Genomic Computing", DataMe – Spanish State Research Agency (TIN2016-80811-P), and OGMIOS – Agència Valenciana de la Innovación, Generalitat Valenciana (INNEST/2021/57).

October 2021

Anna Bernasconi
Arif Canakoglu
Ana León Palacio
José Fabián Reyes Román

The Notion of "System" as a Core Conceptual Modeling Construct for Life Sciences

Roman Lukyanenko[1](✉), Veda C. Storey[2], and Oscar Pastor[3]

[1] HEC Montreal, Montreal, QC, Canada
roman.lukyanenko@hec.ca
[2] Georgia State University, Altanta, GA, USA
vstorey@gsu.edu
[3] PROS Research Center, Universidad Politecnica de Valencia, Valencia, Spain
opastor@dsic.upv.es

Abstract. The understanding of life has always been is a challenge of Life Science. Modeling life implies the need to describe the required details of the systemic structure associated with the working mechanisms of life. In this research, we propose that conceptual modeling can play a crucial role in the modeling of life. Specifically, we introduce the notion of "system" as a separate, and core, conceptual modeling construct and demonstrates how to incorporate it into existing, traditional approaches to conceptual modeling. The work is based on the systemism concept as defined by prior work on ontology. The modeling foundations for systemism are provided and applied to case studies to demonstrate the contributions of the systemic approach over traditional conceptual modeling constructs. In doing so, we provide a high-level approach to modeling systems, which should contribute to dealing with complex systems and structures, such as those generally found in the life sciences.

Keywords: System · Systemism · Conceptual modeling · Life sciences · Conceptual modeling foundations · Complex systems

1 Introduction

Life Science comprises the branches of science that involve the scientific study of life. Understanding life, itself, has always been a major scientific challenge and one that is increasingly important as we seek to understand the complex, global and interconnected world in which we now live. A precise conceptual characterization of the "systems" that are involved in the working mechanisms of life, is, therefore, required. Life Science is a natural context, within which a well-grounded notion of system is crucial. The objective of this research, therefore, is to refine and improve conceptual modeling theory by investigating a thus far overlooked concept of "system". We argue that in the domain of life sciences the concept of "system" should be regarded as a basic conceptual modeling construct.

We propose a set of basic notions that are related to the system construct, position system as a modeling primitive especially applicable in the life sciences domain, explain

© Springer Nature Switzerland AG 2021
I. Reinhartz-Berger and S. Sadiq (Eds.): ER 2021 Workshops, LNCS 13012, pp. 95–103, 2021.
https://doi.org/10.1007/978-3-030-88358-4_8

the limitations of existing modeling languages, and outline research initiatives that could incorporate the system concept.

2 Background: Taking the System for Granted

The notion of a "system" has been omnipresent in information systems development, and, by extension, conceptual modeling. However, it has not been explicitly treated in recognized conceptual modeling languages [1]. Remarkably, if one could ask system engineering experts for a precise definition of a "system," it is most likely that many different definitions would be provided. Indeed, such is the case among scientists as well [2].

Research further assumed that all information technologies are systems; that is, complex objects with interacting parts, which collect, process, store and manipulate information [3, 4]. Furthermore, the domains that are represented in information systems were often understood as *systems*.

A prominent theoretical foundation of conceptual modeling which uses systemic notion is ontology [5, 6]. Ontology is a branch of philosophy that studies what exists in reality, as well as what reality is. One of the most widely studied ontology, the Bunge Wand Weber (BWW) ontology [7], contained the notion of a system. In BWW, "a set of things is a system if, for any bi-partitioning of the set, coupling exist among things in the two subsets" [8].

Many conceptual modeling languages, such as UML class diagrams or extended entity-relationship diagrams, contain constructs such as "part of", that are systemic notions because they deal with complex objects (effectively systems) and their components [9]. Some niche modeling languages provide greater support for systems. Most notably is the Systems Modeling Language (SysML), which is a general-purpose modeling language for systems engineering applications. Although it uses the term "system" as a key notion, it lacks a precise, theoretically grounded definition of what SysML means by a system. The used references to "system" are generic and vague (i.e., it supports the specification, analysis, design, verification and validation of a broad range of systems and systems-of-systems).

Overall, systemic thinking, with its notions related to systems and the concept of a system, is deeply ingrained in the theory and practice of conceptual modeling. At the same time, the construct of the system itself is not explicitly present in popular conceptual modeling approaches. We seek to provide a sound, ontologically supported characterization of the term "system" as a basic construct in conceptual modeling broadly and in the life sciences context, in particular.

3 Rethinking the Nature of Systems in Conceptual Modeling

The fundamental nature of systems can be understood through many theoretical lenses, as systems have been studied extensively in a variety of disciplines. Here we highlight one: a general ontology. Recent advances in ontological theory based on the ideas of Mario Bunge, not only attest to the important ontological status of a system, but also elevate the notion of a system to greater prominence. Mario Bunge is a physicist turned philosopher who made a profound impact on the fields of conceptual modeling, software engineering, information quality, and database design [7, 10]. Much of this influence has been via the BWW ontology, which has made substantial contributions to the theory and practice of IT and conceptual modeling. Among various applications of Bunge's ontology, we highlight one, *Bunge Systemist Ontology (BSO)* [4, 11, 12]. The BSO is a new ontology based on the writings of Bunge later in his life. The ontology positions systems at the very core of existence. Per BSO, Bunge postulates every *thing* is likely a *system,* which is an essential claim, and an ontological primitive of BSO. According to Bunge, and BSO, *the world is made of systems*. BSO provides three explanations of this ontological position.

First, *the notion* of a system allowed Bunge to reason about constituents of reality, which would be difficult to call *things*. For example, the coronavirus pathogenesis pathway, photon's wave-particle duality, the economy of a region, or fields are better called systems. Second, Bunge argued that *there are no simple, structureless entities*. Bunge observed that the history of science teaches us that things, once thought to be irreducible and fundamentally simple (e.g., atom), have later proven to be complex. Bunge [13] concluded *"in tune with a growing suspicion in all scientific quarters* - that there are no simple, structureless entities" (p. 174, emphasis added). For Bunge, this notion is uncontroversial in life sciences domain, where all constituents are systems. Third, Bunge asserted that systemism provides an accurate approach for describing reality. Systemism is a middle ground between individualism (which under-represents internal structures of a system, its relationship with the outer environment, its levels of composition and emergence) and holism (which is not interested in the components and specificity of subsystems).

As suggested in BSO [11], Bunge later offers a broader definition of a system as a "complex object every part or component of which is connected with other parts of the same object in such a manner that the whole possesses some features that its components lack – that is, emergent properties" [2]. We adopt this definition for our analysis.

As captured in BSO [11], different kinds of energy transfer occur in concrete systems, such as mechanical, thermal, kinetic, potential, electric, magnetic, gravitational, chemical [e.g., 27]. Energy transfer leads to change in states of systems, as they acquire or lose their properties, producing what humans conveniently label as *events* and *processes*. As BSO suggests, different kinds of energy can be modeled in conceptual modeling diagrams differently [11]; however, no existing conceptual modeling language to date has a construct to capture these differences.

Bunge suggested that to represent a system, four elements need to be described - Composition, Environment, Structure and Mechanism of the system or the *CESM model*. The *composition* of the system are its components; the *environment*, the external systems with which the system and its subsystems interact; and the *structure*, the relations among its components as well as among these and the environment [15]. Mechanism is defined as "characteristic processes, that make [the system] what it is and the peculiar ways it changes" [14]. To illustrate how to represent systems using CESM, Bunge provides an example of a traditional nuclear family – a type of a socio-biological system [14]:

Its components are the parents and the children; the relevant environment is the immediate physical environment, the neighborhood, and the workplace; the structure is made up of such biological and psychological bonds as love, sharing, and relations with others; and the mechanism consists essentially of domestic chores, marital encounters of various kinds, and child rearing. If the central mechanism breaks down, so does the system as a whole.

Based on CESM, then, system's boundary are those subsystems with directly interact with the environment, whereas those subsystems which only interact with other subsystems of its parent system are the internal components. Thus, we can conclude that just about anything is a system and most definitely every entity in the domain of life sciences is a system.

4   Case of Modeling with Systems in Life Sciences

We use a case study to elaborate on the representational benefits of systems in the domain of life sciences. We first begin with a generic scenario, and then conduct analysis in two scenarios specific to life sciences.

Consider a generic conceptual model that represents two distinct entity types (Spouse and House) and can be instantiated with three different entities (2 real-world spouses and 1 specific house). Adopting a systemist ontology, however, suggests there are numerous systems implied in the model. First, there are at least five systems depicted at the ontological level of the model: the two humans form a social system conventionally called "family"; the two humans and a house form a socioeconomic system called a "household"; finally, there are three separate systems – two humans that are biological systems as well as a house which is a physical system.

At the same time, there are numerous systems which are further implied by our generic conceptual model. These exist at higher or lower ontological levels than the five systems already mentioned. Hence, a biological system (that is, each spouse), in turn, is comprised of further biological systems (e.g., organs, each one of which has its own subsystems, which are cells; cells in turn are complex systems composed of biomolecules such as proteins and nucleic acids; these in-turn can be broken down into atoms, which in-turn are systems). Likewise, the physical system of the house can be broken down into its subsystems, such as rooms, roof and foundation, which in turn are systems. Families and households are themselves subsystems of larger systems, such as communities, cities, countries and societies (as in BSO, we note the issue of infinite recursion related to systems).

In the CESM model, all of these systems can be described in terms of their composition, environment, structure and their mechanisms. This allows us to gain a deeper understanding of the relationship among the focal entities of the domain. Modeling requires to determine a systemic level of description that is frequently done by making an implicit selection decision that fixes the relevant system granularity. Making this decision explicit by delimiting the systemic dimension, allows to clearly delimit the scope of the modeling activity, and to connect different levels of description in order to better understand the working modeling context and to strengthen the modeler purpose.

For example, a household, while composing of three subsystems may have only one system (i.e., head of household) as boundary spanning; that is, a system that directly interacts with the other systems in the environments. This can be important for some real-world applications, such as immigration and refugee services where, for example, in many countries, the interaction between service providers on behalf of the government and the refugee families is commonly conducted through the designated head of the household.

Of course, an argument could be made that conceptual modeling is fundamentally premised on representations with a purpose. We now reuse the same conceptual model, by placing it into a specific realistic context with a defined purpose.

Scenario 1. Application in a Healthcare Setting
In the first scenario, we consider a typical healthcare domain, where the objective is to develop an electronic health record application. This scenario allows us to demonstrate the relationship between systems at different levels. Assume that the initial objective is to keep personal data of a Person (seen as a "patient" in clinical terms) together with a historical record of medical acts that include symptoms, diagnosis and treatments that she has had during her life.

If we consider a Person as a simple entity type, then a simple representation – including the subsequent relationships with other simple entities as Symptoms, Diagnosis and Treatments – is sufficient for a simple conceptual scenario where only such basic conceptualization is needed. However, if we consider a Person from the systemism perspective, a much richer "conceptual universe" emerges, conformed by a hierarchy of systems that would lead to a different level of description depending on the modeler purpose.

We need to apply the system construct if we wish to characterize the Person from a health-oriented perspective and are interested in describing conceptually the structure of his or her genome as a way to view Symptoms, Diagnosis and Treatments as an external representation and a consequence of a much more complex behavior that is the result of the internal genomic structure. Conceptually, the higher-level Person entity type would lead to a more complex, sophisticated system representation that will be dependent on the context (different phenotypes (associated to different diseases) will have different genomic reasons to justify a particular health problem).

As a Patient, a decomposed conceptual model could include a historical perspective describing the higher-level EHR records associated to her health history. This conceptual model should include new entity types that belong to the context being studied. However, a more in-depth conceptual characterization of the systemism dimension of the Person structure is needed if we want to connect the external manifestation of a health problem with its internal, genomic-based metabolic justification. This connection would be based on an associated conceptual model focusing on a genomic-based system perspective (considered as a subsystem of the Person system). Its relevant entity types would be those related to chromosomes, genes, variants, proteins, etc., all of which are adequately connected to their functional environment (e.g. the external manifestation of a health problem) in order to determine pathological situations with clinical implications.

As noted, introducing the system notion allows to conceptually characterize and manage the different system levels of the problem, and their relationships. For instance, the external identification of symptoms (the first level) can be seen as the tip of the iceberg, that reveals the manifestation of a health problem whose explanation is given by its genomic roots. The affected body parts (organs. muscles…) conforms a second system level. The genome sequence obtained from their tissues and other relevant lower-level biological components is the third, more internal, system level.

This systemism perspective can facilitate an adequate data management in the working context of a new medical practice (the modern Medicine of Precision), where a symptom is not just seen as the external perception of a situation, but as the biological result of a particular genomic alteration, that can be detected and identified even without the need of "visualizing" the external effect of the variant problem. This example can show how a BSO-based ontological description of such a Person entity type could lead to design a hierarchy of related conceptual models (from the external, visible "Person" features, to her affected, relevant organs and tissues and to her sequenced genome and its associated metabolic-based behavior). The models are connected by their systemism perspective, thus providing the relevant descriptions at the different levels of detail required by the context of use, all based on a sound ontological background.

Scenario 2. Application in a Foster Care Context
The second scenario is a foster care application, which enables us to discuss the challenge of modeling system components, as opposed to systemic layers. Assume the objective is to develop a decision support system for foster care managers (e.g., [16–18]). The foster care managers are tasked with protecting the health, safety, and well-being of the children and with providing support to foster and adoptive parents through case management services. A decision support system in this context would capture essential information about the adoptive families.

In this scenario, we retain the 3 entity types of the generic scenario because they now represent an adoptive household candidate. For simplicity, assume a household has two parents (represented by the Spouse entity types) and a single house where a child is going to live should the case be positively determined for this household. Many requisite details now need to be added to our model. For example, we would need to add particular attributes of the spouses and the house, the foster care managers need to consider when making the placement decision. Hence, we can indicate the dates of birth of each spouse, their name, occupation, individual income. For house, in a foster care scenario, typical attributes of interest include the size of the house, the kinds of equipment and amenities available, the number of rooms, the occupancy load and the occupancy availability, among other elements. This additional information can be seamlessly captured with existing conceptual modeling symbols (e.g., additional entity types).

However, many additional pieces of information which relate to systems in the domain, would be more challenging to represent. Some relevant aspects of the domain could be represented, but it would be cumbersome to do due to the *lack of systemic constructs* in common modeling grammars. Systems commonly have systemic or emergent properties. A particularly important system for the healthcare domain is that of a household, comprised of the spouses and the house and that of a family which includes the two spouses, but excludes the house. Each of the system have unique emergent properties. Systemic properties of the household include *household income, designated head of household, length of time household existed* and *household type* (e.g., nucleus, nucleus with relatives) – all major determinants of family's eligibility for adoption. The attributes of the family are different and include *date of marriage, joint property titles* (e.g., car title), *joint financial obligations*. To model these emergent properties, an analyst needs to create two additional entities, *Household* and *Family*, and indicate the attributes for each, as well as the relationship to our existing entities. The resulting model becomes quite complex, even in its simplified form, lacking attributes and relationship names. A representation of just two systems using conventional conceptual modeling approaches, results in a proliferation of the relationships, because existing entity types need to be related to these systems to indicate their part of relationships. Another potential limitation of using traditional modeling constructs is a relative difficulty to discern the nested relationship of the systems. Finally, if we assume that the spouses and the house are atomic entities, whereas family and household are systems, we have a case of construct overload. Construct overload occurs when the same construct (in this case, entity), is used to represent two different real-world constructs (i.e., atomic entity versus system).

Furthermore, modern conceptual modeling grammars lack an ability to represent the mechanism element of systems (based on the CESM). A mechanism shows recurring patterns of activities among the components of a system. Such activities capture causal relationships and patterns of interaction. For example, in the foster care scenario, this could be family specific patterns and pre-existing agreements, such as, if one spouse loses a job, the other spouse picks up a temporary second job on the side, hence ensuring adequate support for the foster child. Such a pattern can be easily represented using a variety of process modeling notations (e.g., BPMN, EPC). However, there is no practice of referencing fragments of such models directly from a conceptual data model. To faithfully represent CESM, a system construct would have to be linked with a fragment process modeling construct – a new notion for conceptual modeling practice.

5 Discussion: Systemism for Life Sciences

The implicit treatment of systems has many limitations because it ignores the fundamental ontological status of systems in reality. However, based on the three scenarios we can suggest several benefits of introducing systems into common conceptual modeling grammars: reduction of diagrammatic complexity, avoidance of construct overload, increased model comprehensibility and increased model expressiveness. These benefits especially provide utility to life sciences, as our scenarios have demonstrated. In life sciences, systems are not simply the context within which information technologies are based, or specific kinds of objects that contain parts. Rather, they are the ontological primitives upon which, one could argue, other conceptual modeling constructs can be built. This suggests that at least the domain of life sciences can greatly benefit from explicit modeling of systems with a provision of a dedicated "system" construct.

Naturally, representing a system involves more than simply identifying the component parts, as presently supported by popular conceptual modeling languages, such as UML. Systems indeed appear to require a dedicated representation. For example, Bunge proposed the CESM model, which is also incorporated into the BSO ontology. It is reasonable to assume, and subsequently analyze, how this model could provide a design template for representing systems. Doing so would require additional design work in conceptual modeling to determine how to incorporate the CESM model into conceptual modeling diagrams. Then, research needs to consider the complexity of the diagrams so that the introduction of additional elements is clearly identified and effective visual representation of the elements of the model, created.

Accepting the merit of using a dedicated system construct, implies that existing conceptual modeling languages may be enriched through an addition of a dedicated system symbol. For example, the entity-relationship diagram [19] may now include another major construct, that is, a *system*, making it a diagram which represents atomic entity types, attributes, relationships and system types. A possible representation for a system could be a dashed box surrounding the entity types that are deemed as components or parts of the system.

The addition of the system construct leads to the rethinking of the ontological status of the entity. Once system is added as a meta-model entity, it can be understood as an atomic, simple object. Future research is needed to investigate similar extensions to existing conceptual modeling languages. These efforts could also consider how to represent instances of system, that is concrete systems (as opposed to kinds of systems). This would contribute to the recent debates about representation of instances, which thus far assumed atomic objects [20, 21].

6   Conclusions

Unravelling the secrets of human conditions and diseases is a major challenge in the domain of life sciences. To achieve it, a precise ontological characterization of the relevant components of complex biological processes is required. This paper contributes with the proposal of a well-grounded ontological notion of system as a basic modeling unit intended to support modeling of biological processes.

References

1. Recker, J., Lukyanenko, R., Sabegh, M.A., Samuel, B.M., Castellanos, A.: From representation to mediation: a new agenda for conceptual modeling research in a digital world. MIS Q. **45**, 269–300 (2021)
2. Bunge, M.A.: Finding Philosophy in Social Science. Yale University Press, New Haven, CT (1996)
3. Checkland, P., Holwell, S.: Information, Systems, and Information Systems: Making Sense of the Field. John Wiley & Sons Inc., Hoboken, NJ (1998)
4. Lukyanenko, R.: A journey to BSO: evaluating earlier and more recent ideas of Mario Bunge as a foundation for information and software development. In: Exploring Modeling Methods for Systems Analysis and Development (EMMSAD 2020), pp. 1–15. Grenoble, France (2020)
5. Guarino, N., Guizzardi, G., Mylopoulos, J.: On the philosophical foundations of conceptual models. Inf. Model. Knowl. Bases **31**, 1 (2020)
6. Guizzardi, G.: Ontological foundations for structural conceptual models. Telematics Instituut Fundamental Research Series, Enschede, The Netherlands (2005)
7. Wand, Y., Weber, R.: Thirty years later: some reflections on ontological analysis in conceptual modeling. J. Database Manag. (JDM). **28**, 1–17 (2017)

8. Wand, Y., Weber, R.: On the ontological expressiveness of information systems analysis and design grammars. Inf. Syst. J. **3**, 217–237 (1993)
9. Wand, Y., Storey, V.C., Weber, R.: An ontological analysis of the relationship construct in conceptual modeling. ACM Trans. Database Syst. **24**, 494–528 (1999)
10. Burton-Jones, A., Green, P., Parsons, J., Siau, K.: Special issue on ontological analysis in conceptual modeling, Part 2. J. Database Manag. **28**, i–x (2017)
11. Lukyanenko, R., Storey, V.C., Pastor, O.: Foundations of information technology based on Bunge's systemist philosophy of reality. Softw. Syst. Model. **20**(4), 921–938 (2021)
12. Castellanos, A., Lukyanenko, R., Storey, V.C.: Modeling observational crowdsourcing. In: ER Forum 2020, pp. 1–8. Vienna, Austria (2020)
13. Bunge, M.A.: Philosophy of Science: Volume 2, From Explanation to Justification. Routledge, New York NY (2017)
14. Bunge, M.A.: Chasing Reality: Strife Over Realism. University of Toronto Press, Toronto (2006)
15. Bunge, M.A.: Treatise on Basic Philosophy: Ontology II: A World of Systems. Reidel Publishing Company, Boston, MA (1979)
16. Becker, M.A., Jordan, N., Larsen, R.: Predictors of successful permanency planning and length of stay in foster care: the role of race, diagnosis and place of residence. Child Youth Serv. Rev. **29**, 1102–1113 (2007)
17. Lukyanenko, R., Castellanos, A., Parsons, J., Chiarini Tremblay, M., Storey, V.C.: How conceptual modeling can support machine learning: evidence from foster care. In: Cappiello, C., Ruiz, M. (eds.) Special Interest Group in Systems Analysis and Design (SIGSAND), pp. 1–11. New York, NY, USA (2019)
18. Castellanos, A., Castillo, A., Tremblay, M.C., Lukyanenko, R., Parsons, J., Storey, V.C.: Improving machine learning performance using conceptual modeling. In: AAAI Symposium on Combining Machine Learning and Knowledge Engineering in Practice, pp. 1–4. Stanford, CA (2021)
19. Chen, P.: The entity-relationship model - toward a unified view of data. ACM Trans. Database Syst. **1**, 9–36 (1976)
20. Lukyanenko, R., Parsons, J., Samuel, B.M.: Representing instances: the case for reengineering conceptual modeling grammars. Eur. J. Inf. Syst. **28**, 68–90 (2019). https://doi.org/10.1080/0960085X.2018.1488567
21. Eriksson, O., Johannesson, P., Bergholtz, M.: The case for classes and instances-a response to representing instances: the case for reengineering conceptual modelling grammars. Eur. J. Inf. Syst. **28**, 681–693 (2019)

Characterization and Treatment of the Temporal Dimension of Genomic Variations: A Conceptual Model-Based Approach

Alberto García Simón[(✉)] [iD], Mireia Costa Sánchez, and Oscar Pastor [iD]

PROS Research Center, Universitat Politècnica de València,
Camí de Vera, s/n, 46022 València, Spain
{algarsi3,opastor}@pros.upv.es, micossan@etsii.upv.es

Abstract. The reclassification of the genomic variation's pathogenicity is not a rare event, and it may have dramatic consequences on a patient's diagnosis and treatment. In this work, we present a characterization of the temporal dimension concept regarding the variation's reclassification. Following this, we have expanded this characterization to include other dimensions of genomics that can also change over time. This characterization allows identifying what dimensions change, why they change, and how we can deal with these changes. On the other hand, this characterization has been the base to develop a conceptual based-approach that has let us solve the problems regarding the temporal dimension in a real-world, specific working context.

Keywords: Temporal dimension · Conceptual models · SILE method · Delfos platform

1 Introduction

The practice of medicine is currently undergoing a paradigm shift towards disease prevention and individualized treatment, where *Precision medicine* has emerged as a promising approach to achieve these goals. According to [3], precision medicine is a computational approach that integrates and interprets *omics* data to treat every patient as an individual case. In precision medicine, identifying relevant genomic variations that are associated to diseases with high-quality evidence is key for providing efficient prevention, diagnosis, and treatment.

This identification process uses several databases that store variations and their associations with diseases. However, clinicians struggle when working with them. There are multiple reasons causing this situation, from which we can mention the following: i) the huge volume of publicly available data [13], ii) the complexity of integrating omics data [4], iii) the complexity of dealing with the quality issues that are inherent to genomic data [10], or iv) the reclassification of variations' pathogenicity over time [2], among others.

© Springer Nature Switzerland AG 2021
I. Reinhartz-Berger and S. Sadiq (Eds.): ER 2021 Workshops, LNCS 13012, pp. 104–113, 2021.
https://doi.org/10.1007/978-3-030-88358-4_9

This work focuses on the latter, namely, **the reclassification of variations' pathogenicity over time**. To this purpose, we present a characterization of the notion of **temporal dimension** regarding the reclassification of variant's pathogenicity. Following this, we expand the scope of the research to characterize other dimensions of the genomic variants that may be affected by the temporal dimension. To perform this characterization, we have identified **which genomic concepts change over time**, **why do they change**, and **how to deal with these changes**. Finally, we present a conceptual model-based approach that intends to solve the temporal dimension problem in a specific working context.

The remainder of this work is structured as follows: Sect. 2 motivates the need for this work. Section 3 specifies the context of this research. Section 4 presents our conceptual model-based solution. Section 5 discusses how generalizable our solution is along with its potential benefits. Finally, Sect. 6 reports our conclusions.

2 Motivation

The ultimate goal of precision medicine is *to deliver the right treatment, at the right time, every time to the right person*. However, the high variability of the genomics information over time has important consequences that complicate achieving this goal. The reasons behind this situation are complex and diverse [13,14], but the reclassification of variations' pathogenicity over time is one of them. Although there is few published data quantifying the prevalence of reclassification [8], the existing evidence indicates that variant reclassification over time is not a rare event [11]. Variant reclassification can have dramatic consequences depending on the affected disease. For example, variant reclassification is commonplace in hereditary cancer predisposition testing [12], which has a psychosocial impact on individuals and affects family communication [15]. Another example is found in the diagnosis of inherited arrhythmogenic syndromes, where 70% of rare genetic variations associated with these syndromes have been reclassified over time [1].

Besides variants, the significance of other genomic components changes over time. For example, genes. The American College of Medical Genetics and Genomics (ACMG) recommended conducting genomics studies on a set of 56 genes in 2013, but this list has been expanded with 13 additional genes in 2021 [9].

3 Definition of the Context

The characterization of the reclassification of variations' pathogenicity over time is too complex to be fully addressed in only one paper. Thus, we have narrowed it down to a specific working use case whose ultimate goal is to identify variations that are relevant and have strong supporting evidence. Two core elements support achieving this goal, namely, the SILE method and the Delfos platform.

3.1   The SILE Method

The SILE method, provides researchers with an artifact to search for reliable data sources (**S**earch), identify relevant information in them (**I**dentify), store it adequately (**L**oad), and exploit it (**E**xploitation).

The method has a solid ontological background that is provided by the Conceptual Schema of the Genome (CSG). The CSG allows creating conceptual views with a subset of the most relevant concepts regarding the working use case [5]. These views are generated using the ISGE method, which is described in [6]. Figure 1 shows the conceptual view that is used in the SILE method, which we call the Conceptual Schema of the Genome in Delfos (CSGD).

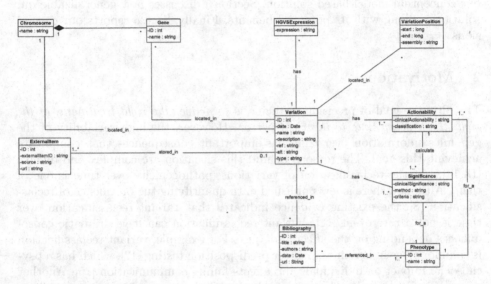

Fig. 1. The Conceptual Schema of the Genome in Delfos (CSGD).

The central entity of the CSGD is the VARIATION class. A variation is defined by the reference and the alternative alleles, the variation type, and the last time it was analyzed by the SILE method. The references of variations in external data bases are modeled in the conceptual schema with the EXTERNALITEM class.

The location of a variation is represented in three ways: the CHROMOSOME where the variation is located, the set of GENES where the variation is located, and the position of the variation (VARIATIONPOSITION class) in the complete genome for a specific sequencing ASSEMBLY.

Variations are linked to phenotypes through a set of clinical SIGNIFICANCES that represent the pathogenicity (i.e. pathogenic or benign) of a variation regarding a phenotype. The different significances are provided by researchers, who submit the result of their work. Additionally, we have created the ACTIONABIL-ITY class, which is characterized by the clinical actionablity [7], an aggregated value of the significances that represents the practical importance of the variant for a phenotype, and the variant's classification, that represents the quality of the evidence that supports such actionability.

Finally, each variation can contain phenotype-related BIBLIOGRAPHY, represented by the Bibliography class.

3.2 The DELFOS Oracle

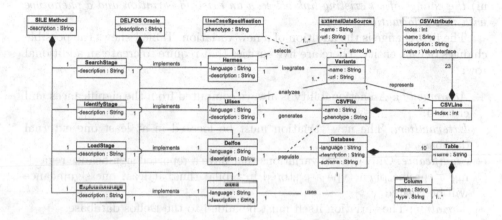

Fig. 2. Simplified diagram of the components of the DELFOS oracle.

The DELFOS oracle is the platform that automates the SILE method. It is composed of four modules, one per SILE method stage. The first module is called Hermes, and it automatizes the Search stage of SILE with a R package that is responsible of extracting the variations' information for a set of selected data sources and integrate it. The second module is called Ulises, and it automatizes the Identify stage with an R package that is used to classify variations according to its relevance on the clinical field. This module generates a CSV file with the classified variations. The third module is Delfos, and it automatizes the Load Stage with a MySQL database and a web-based service. The database instantiates the conceptual schema shown in Fig. 1. The fourth module is called Sibila, and it automatizes the Exploitation stage with a web-based Genome Information System that connects to the Delfos' database. Figure 2 shows a simplified vision of the DELFOS oracle, that includes all the mentioned modules.

4 Characterizing the Temporal Dimension

After presenting the context of this research, we present the characterization of the temporal dimension, which is the core contribution of our work. In Sect. 4.1, we identify what elements of the CSGD can change over time and the reasons why they change. In Sect. 4.2, we present our solution.

4.1   Variability over Time

To study the variability of the genomic variant's information over time (i.e. the temporal dimension), we have carried a study to identify what changes occurred over time on the genomic information related to two specific phenotypes: Early Onset Alzheimer's Disease and Cystic Fibrosis. After analyzing the study results, we identified three types of data changes: i) *the addition of a new variation*, ii) *the addition of a new link between an existing variation and a phenotype*, and iii) *the change of an existing link between an existing variation and a phenotype with new information*.

The first change is the addition of a new variation. Table 1 shows the possible changes of each entity. There are five entities that require to create an additional row:

- *Actionability*: An actionability is always computed from the significances and created.
- *ExternalItem*: The new variation must be located in at least one external database.
- *Significance*: Only genetic variations that have a reported significance regarding a specific phenotype are stored in Sibila; thus, at least one significance will be created.
- *Variation*: The variation itself must be added to the Delfos database.

Besides, there are four entities whose creation is optional:

- *Bibliography*: There are variations that has no associated bibliography.
- *Gene*: If the gene that is affected by the variation already exists in the database, no changes are needed.
- *HGVSExpression*: There are variations that do not have HGVS expression
- *Phenotype*: If the phenotype that is affected by the variation already exists in the database, no changes are needed.
- *VariantPosition*: There are variations whose location in the DNA is unknown.

Table 1. Actions when a new variation is included in the database.

Entity	Create Action	Delete Action	Update Action
Actionability	Yes (Mandatory)	No	No
Bibliography	Yes (Optional)	No	No
ExternalItem	Yes (Mandatory)	No	No
Gene	Yes (Optional)	No	No
HGVSExpression	Yes (Optional)	No	No
Phenotype	Yes (Optional)	No	No
Significance	Yes (Mandatory)	No	No
Variation	Yes (Mandatory)	No	No
VariationPosition	Yes (Optional)	No	No

The second change is the *addition of a new link between an existing variation and a phenotype*. This change is triggered when a new link between a variation that already exists in the database and a phenotype is found. Table 2 shows the possible changes of each entity:

- *Actionability*: If a new link is added, then the actionability must be recalculated.
- *Bibliography*: New bibliography may be generated to justify the new link between the variation and the phenotype.
- *ExternalItem*: Additional databases containing an existing variation may be included over time, and previous database can be deleted. Besides, the identifier or URL of a variation in a database can also change over time.
- *Gene*: Overlapping genes exist in the genome. An existing variation can be located in a newly discovered gene (which overlaps an existing one) that is of interest for a phenotype. In this situation, the new gene must be created.
- *HGVSExpression*: New HGVS expressions can appear while others can be deleted.
- *phenotype*: If the new phenotype does not exist, it is included in the database.
- *Significance*: Just like in Table 1, at least one significance will be created when a new link between a variation and a phenotype is established.
- *Variation*: Some aspects of the existing variation can be updated.
- *VariantPosition*: Over time, new assemblies can be generated and included as a new position of a variation. Besides, a previously variation with unknown position in the DNA sequence can be properly identified and located.

Table 2. Actions when a new link between an existing variation and a phenotype is included in the database.

Entity	Create Action	Delete Action	Update Action
Actionability	Yes (Mandatory)	No	No
Bibliography	Yes (Optional)	No	No
ExternalItem	Yes (Optional)	Yes (Optional)	Yes (Optional)
Gene	Yes (Optional)	No	No
HGVSExpression	Yes (Optional)	Yes (Optional)	No
Phenotype	No	No	No
Significance	Yes (Mandatory)	No	No
Variation	No	No	Yes (Optional)
VariationPosition	Yes (Optional)	No	No

The third change is the *change of an existing link between a variation and a phenotype with new information*, and it is triggered when some aspect or quality of a link between a variation and a phenotype is modified in the CSV file. Table 3 shows the possible changes of each entity:

- *Actionability*: The actionability of a variation for a phenotype can change if the set of significances used to compute its value changes.
- *Bibliography*: New bibliography can be generated to represent new knowledge in the domain regarding an existing link between a variation and a phenotype.
- *ExternalItem*: Additional databases containing an existing variation can be included over time. Previously selected databases can be deleted for multiple reasons. Besides, the identifier or url of a variation in a database can change over time also.
- *Gene*: The role of genes in the expression of phenotypes is an ever-changing matter of study. A gene that was not identified as a gene of interest for a phenotype can change this qualification. The gene that becomes of interest for a phenotype can contain an existing variation. In this situation, the new gene must be created.
- *HGVSExpression*: New HGVS expressions can appear while others can be deleted.
- *phenotype*: The phenotype cannot be modified because it already exists in the database.
- *Significance*: The set of significances can change over time.
- *Variation*: Some aspects of the existing variation can be updated.
- *VariantPosition*: Over time, new assemblies can be generated and included as a new position of a variation. Besides, a previously variation with unknown position in the DNA sequence can be properly identified and located.

Table 3. Actions when an existing link between a variation and a phenotype is updated in the database.

Entity	Create Action	Delete Action	Update Action
Actionability	No	No	Yes (Optional)
Bibliography	Yes (Optional)	No	No
ExternalItem	Yes (Optional)	Yes (Optional)	Yes (Optional)
Gene	Yes (Optional)	No	No
HGVSExpression	Yes (Optional)	Yes (Optional)	No
Phenotype	Yes (Optional)	No	No
Significance	Yes (Optional)	Yes (Optional)	Yes (Optional)
Variation	No	No	Yes (Optional)
VariationPosition	Yes (Optional)	No	No

4.2   The Solution

Once we have characterized all the changes that affect the genomic variant's information, we describe how we manage the temporal dimension on the Delfos platform. First, the we present the changes carried out to consider the temporal dimension in the simplified diagram of Fig. 3. Then, we present the characterization of the temporal dimension in the SILE method.

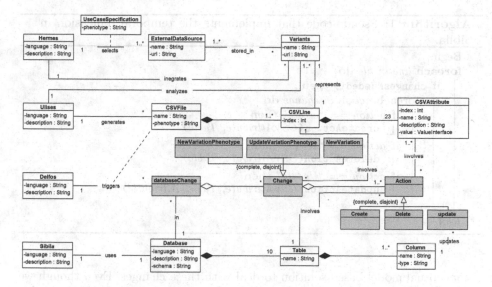

Fig. 3. A characterization of the temporal dimension in the SILE method.

When we execute Ulises, a new CSV file with the most up-to-date information regarding the variations of a specific phenotype is generated. This file is composed of 23 columns, and each of them is mapped to either a specific attribute of a class of the conceptual schema of Fig. 1.

On the other hand, when we execute Delfos, it loads into the database this CSV file. If new data is detected during the execution of this process, a DATABASE CHANGE is triggered. Generally speaking, a DATABASE CHANGE is a multi-step process that is composed of at least one CHANGE in the database. At most, one change of the three changes described on Sect. 4.1 can occur per CSV line. Each one of these changes is composed of a set of atomic actions, being them triggered by a specific attribute of the CSV line that caused the change. Thus, an action involves a specific attribute of the CSV file and a table of the database where the file is imported. There are three types of actions regarding the CSV file: to create a new row, to delete an existing row, or to edit an attribute of an existing row of the table that is affected. In the case of an update, the attribute to be updated is indicated also through the *updates* relationship. Algorithm 1 shows the pseudo-code of how to update the Sibila database based on the information reported above. The amount of tables and attributes that can change is limited by the classes of the conceptual schema used to develop Sibila.

5   Discussion

In this work, we have been able to characterize the variability of the genomic variant's information over time. Based on this characterization, we have presented

Algorithm 1: Pseudo-code that implements the temporal dimension in Sibila.

```
Begin;
foreach line in file do
    if changesNeeded() then
        foreach action in change do
            if action == "create" then
                createAction(CSVAttribute, Table)
            if action == "delete" then
                deleteAction(CSVAttribute, Table)
            if action == "Update" then
                updateAction(CSVAttribute, Table, Attributte)
End;
```

a conceptual model-based solution to deal with these changes. Even though we have focused on a specific case (i.e., the genomic variant's information), this approach is generalizable to other use cases and domains.

The characterization exercise and the conceptual model-based solution presented in this work constitute a valuable outcome in a precision medicine context. Changes over time in the genomic variant's information, and other genomic data, may affect past, present, and future diagnosis and treatments, having a considerable impact on a patient's health. The first step to deal with the temporal dimension of genomic information is to characterize the changes occurring over time. Thus, our work constitutes an important step towards dealing with the temporal dimension in such a critical context as clinical care.

6   Conclusions

Characterizing the temporal dimensions in genomics is complex, having a direct impact on patients' diagnosis and treatment. This context justifies the relevance of this work. We have proposed a new step towards managing the impact of the temporal dimension in genomics data correctly. Our conceptual model-based solution allows Delfos to correctly manage all the changes that occur in genomics over time. This ensures that the temporal dimension is now properly handled. With this approach, the Delfos platform will be able to offer clinical experts the most current information for present clinical care and past diagnoses and treatments that may need to be reviewed.

References

1. Campuzano, O., et al.: Reanalysis and reclassification of rare genetic variants associated with inherited arrhythmogenic syndromes. EBioMedicine **54**, 102732 (2020). https://doi.org/10.1016/j.ebiom.2020.102732

2. Costa, M., León, A., Pastor, O.: The importance of the temporal dimension in identifying relevant genomic variants: a case study. In: Grossmann, G., Ram, S. (eds.) Advances in Conceptual Modeling. ER 2020. Lecture Notes in Computer Science, vol. 12584, pp. 51–60. Springer, Cham (2020). https://doi.org/10.1007/978-3-030-65847-2_5

3. Duffy, D.J.: Problems, challenges and promises: perspectives on precision medicine. Brief. Bioinform. **17**(3), 494–504 (2016). https://doi.org/10.1093/bib/bbv060

4. Galvão, J., Leon, A., Costa, C., Santos, M.Y., López, Ó.P.: Automating data integration in adaptive and data-intensive information systems. In: Themistocleous, M., Papadaki, M., Kamal, M.M. (eds.) EMCIS 2020. LNBIP, vol. 402, pp. 20 34. Springer, Cham (2020). https://doi.org/10.1007/978-3-030-63396-7_2

5. García S., A., Casamayor, J.C.: Towards the generation of a species-independent conceptual schema of the genome. In: Grossmann, G., Ram, S. (eds.) Advances in Conceptual Modeling. ER 2020. Lecture Notes in Computer Science, vol. 12584, pp. 61–70. Springer, Cham (2020). https://doi.org/10.1007/978-3-030-65847-2_6

6. García S., A., Casamayor, J.C., Pastor, O.: ISGE: a conceptual model-based method to correctly manage genome data. In: Nurcan, S., Korthaus, A. (eds.) CAiSE 2021. LNBIP, vol. 424, pp. 47–54. Springer, Cham (2021). https://doi.org/10.1007/978-3-030-79108-7_6

7. León, A., García S., A., Costa, M., Vañó Ribelles, A., Pastor, O.: Evolution of an adaptive information system for precision medicine. In: Nurcan, S., Korthaus, A. (eds.) CAiSE 2021. LNBIP, vol. 424, pp. 3–10. Springer, Cham (2021). https://doi.org/10.1007/978-3-030-79108-7_1

8. Mersch, J.: Prevalence of variant reclassification following hereditary cancer genetic testing. JAMA **320**(12), 1266–1274 (2018). https://doi.org/10.1001/jama.2018.13152

9. Miller, D.T., et al.: ACMG SF v3.0 list for reporting of secondary findings in clinical exome and genome sequencing: a policy statement of the American College of Medical Genetics and Genomics (ACMG). Genetics in Medicine, pp. 1–10. Nature Publishing Group (May 2021). https://doi.org/10.1038/s41436-021-01172-3

10. Palacio, A.L., López, O.P.: Smart data for genomic information systems: the SILE method. Complex Syst. Inform. Model. Q. (17), 1–23 (2018). https://doi.org/10.7250/csimq.2018-17.01

11. Plon, S.E., Rehm, H.L.: The ancestral pace of variant reclassification. JNCI J. Natl. Cancer Inst. **110**(10), 1133–1134 (2018). https://doi.org/10.1093/jnci/djy075

12. Slavin, T.P., et al.: The effects of genomic germline variant reclassification on clinical cancer care. Oncotarget **10**(4), 417–423 (2019). https://doi.org/10.18632/oncotarget.26501

13. Stephens, Z.D.: Big data: astronomical or genomical? PLOS Biol. **13**(7), e1002195. Public Library of Science (2015). https://doi.org/10.1371/journal.pbio.1002195

14. Vihinen, M.: Problems in variation interpretation guidelines and in their implementation in computational tools. Mole. Genet. Genomic Med. **8**(9), e1206 (2020). https://doi.org/10.1002/mgg3.1206

15. Wong, E.K., et al.: Perceptions of genetic variant reclassification in patients with inherited cardiac disease. Eur. J. Hum. Genet. **27**(7), 1134–1142. Nature Publishing Group (2019). https://doi.org/10.1038/s41431-019-0377-6

Extension of the Genomic Conceptual Model to Integrate Genome-Wide Association Studies

Federico Comolli[(✉)]

Department of Electronics, Information and Bioengineering,
Politecnico di Milano, Milan, Italy
`federico1.comolli@mail.polimi.it`

Abstract. The first human genome has been sequenced at the turn of the year 2000. Since then, modern biology has made great progresses, also thanks to the introduction of Next-generation sequencing in the mid-2000s. The growing availability of genomic data led to the birth of tertiary analysis, concerning sense-making and extraction of useful biological information. To deal with data heterogeneity, in the last decade many tools have been introduced to achieve genomic data integration: among them, the Genomic Conceptual Model (GCM) and the META-BASE architecture. The latter one allows to map data from many projects into the GCM through an integration pipeline.

In this work, we proposed an extension of the GCM to integrate two additional sources into the META-BASE architecture, namely: GWAS Catalog (curated by the NHGRI and EBI institutes) and FinnGen (curated by the University of Helsinki). These two sources host Genome-Wide Association Studies (GWAS), useful for explaining the connection between genome variations of single nucleotides and particular traits. They are organized according to different data models but share the same data semantics. As a result of our integration efforts, we enable the interoperable use and querying of GWAS datasets with several other genomic datasets (including TCGA, ENCODE, Roadmap Epigenomics, 1000 Genomes Project, and GENCODE).

Keywords: Data integration · Genomic datasets · Bioinformatics · Multiomics studies · GWAS

1   Introduction

Since the mid-2000s, thanks to the introduction of Next-generation sequencing [22], a whole human DNA sequence can be read in a short time and in a cheap way. After being sequenced, the so-called *tertiary analysis* [21] is performed, dealing with sense-making of the huge amount of data produced by the previous analysis. Big amount of data collected by different consortia need to be integrated to allow scientists to extract information useful to understand how life is orchestrated by the DNA and how the sequence of nucleotides affects diseases or phenotype. Data

© Springer Nature Switzerland AG 2021
I. Reinhartz-Berger and S. Sadiq (Eds.): ER 2021 Workshops, LNCS 13012, pp. 114–124, 2021.
https://doi.org/10.1007/978-3-030-88358-4_10

produced in the context of different projects have different formats, resulting into an obstacle for data interoperability required by the tertiary analysis [1].

A big effort to cope with genomic data heterogeneity has been performed by the GeCo project of Politecnico di Milano developing a conceptual model (the Genomic Conceptual Model [3]), a query language (the GenoMetric Query Language [14]) and a pipeline to integrate genomic data from multiple sources (the META-BASE architecture [2]). One of the purposes of the GeCo project has been to create an integrated genomic repository that collects data from major consortia around the world (e.g., 1000 Genomes [24], Cistrome [29], ENCODE [25], GEN-CODE [9], Roadmap Epigenomics [12], and TCGA [28] by means of OpenGDC [7]).

In this article, we presented the modelling efforts spent to integrate into the META-BASE architecture a new class of studies called Genome-Wide Association Studies (GWAS). They involve testing genetic variants across the genomes of many individuals to identify genotype-phenotype associations. By comparing groups of people affected by a disease or trait (cases) and without it (controls), the outcomes of these studies comprise the more frequent nucleotides in the cases group against the controls. The difference of GWAS from other studies is the focus of the analysis: single nucleotide polymorphisms (SNPs) for GWAS, whole portions of genome or DNA features for other omics studies. GWAS have revolutionized the field of complex disease genetics over the past decade, providing numerous compelling associations for human complex traits and diseases [23]. Examples of GWAS are [26], which identified 103 SNPs associated to "schizophrenia", and [11], which found 333 SNPs associated to "multiple sclerosis". This work focuses on two GWAS repositories, namely the GWAS Catalog [5] and the FinnGen Project [8].

Integrating multiple omic repositories (i.e., genomic, proteomic and transcriptomic) into the GCM serves to improve the knowledge about the molecular function and disease etiology. Multi-omic studies combine different biological entities to find novel associations between them, paving the road for disease treatments and prevention. The work in this paper focuses on the integration made on metadata describing experiments, rather than on the genomic region attributes, whose transformation is trivial (see [13]).

2   Related Works

Due to the ongoing increase of genomic data, the management techniques for large data can be applied to address the heterogeneity and complexity of the biological field. Many works exploit the conceptual modeling to capture the diverse biological objects and to interpret their relationships (see [16–20,27]). The objective of the cited works is to support biologists to extract insights from raw genomic data. The Genomic Conceptual Model [3], whose extension is introduced in this article, goes further the description and data organization of complex biological integrated repositories; it is an architecture driving the integration of new genomic repositories. The work presented in this article exemplifies how the architecture can be exploited to integrate new datasets, mapping them to a shared conceptual model.

3 Background

A shared conceptual schema, the Genomic Conceptual Model (GCM), has been introduced to describe semantically heterogeneous data. Multiple genomic sources have been mapped over the GCM following the META-BASE pipeline, by extracting and transforming the source-specific metadata.

The GCM is an entity-relationship model used to gather metadata of heterogeneous genomic data sources. It is organized as a star-schema centered on the `Item` entity from which depart four sub-schemata (or views), recalling a classic star-schema organization that is typical of data warehouses; they respectively describe biological, technological, management and extraction aspects (more thoroughly described in [3]):

- *Central Entity*: it represents an elementary experimental file of genomic regions and their attributes. Files are typically used by biologists for data extraction, analysis and visualization operations.
- *Biological View*: it consists of the chain of entities `Item-Replicate-Biosample-Donor`, representing the biological elements that contribute to the `Item` production. The `Donor` represents an individual (characterized by Age, Gender and Ethnicity) or strain of a specific organism (Species) from which the biological material was derived or the cell line was established.
- *Technology View*: it describes the technology used to produce the data `Item`. An `Item` is associated by means of a one-to-many relationship with a given `ExperimentType`.
- *Management View*: it consists of the chain of entities `Item-Case-Project` describing the organizational process for the production of items.
- *Extraction View*: it includes the entity `Dataset`, used to describe common properties of homogeneous items.

4 Data Design

Samples of the typical integrated sources are assigned to single individuals; for each biological sample we can retrieve the information about the donor(s) who provided it. Instead, Genome-Wide Association Studies are based on *cohorts of patients*, so the considered granularity is coarser w.r.t. already integrated datasets. For each GWAS sample we know the cohort size and limited ancestral information, while detailed information about each single component of the cohort is not available. For this reason, in order to include the two sources GWAS Catalog and FinnGen into the META-BASE repository, we have extended the GCM introducing the *GWAS View*, to meet the constraints of the considered class of studies.

Figure 1 illustrates the extended GCM with two added entities, i.e., `Cohort` and `Ancestry`, belonging to the *GWAS View*. In the following, we describe this novel view for including GWAS samples.

Entity Item. It is the central entity of the GCM and it is shared between all its views. A GWAS `Item` contains all the SNPs associated with the phenotype under

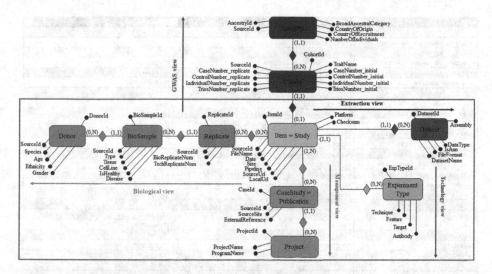

Fig. 1. Extended Genomic Conceptual Model. With respect to its original version (enclosed in the rectangle), it contains a new view (the *GWAS View*). When it gathers GWAS data, the *Biological View* remains empty (optional relationship between `Item` and `Replicate`); on the opposite when receiving different classes of studies, the *GWAS View* stays empty (optional relationship between `Item` and `Cohort`).

consideration. It contains metadata useful to describe how the corresponding region file (list of SNPs) is produced.

Entity Cohort. Each `Item` of the GCM has its corresponding `Cohort` which includes the information about the groups of people from which the biological sample is collected. An `Item` is obtained by comparing the DNA sequences of the cases (people affected by the phenotype) against the controls (people not showing that phenotype). Moreover, a sample can have one initial stage and one or more replicate stages. Some GWA studies, besides cases and controls, can be based upon groups of individuals or trios. The entity `Cohort` holds the cardinalities of the cases, controls, individuals or trios that provide the corresponding `Item`, both of the initial stage or replicate stage(s). Among all its metadata, the attribute "TraitName" is most relevant as GWA studies are driven by a phenotype (or trait, endpoint, disease).

Entity Ancestry. A `Cohort` can be partitioned into many `Ancestries`, each one containing given ancestral information about the current partition. The country of origin, the ancestral category or the country from which the participants are selected are possible available information about a partition.

Figure 2 shows how the source-specific metadata of GWAS Catalog and FinnGen are mapped into the attributes of the GCM: in the left column we list the attributes of the GCM, in the central column we report the attributes of GWAS Catalog, while in the right column we provide the attributes of FinnGen. The metadata enclosed by quotes are meant to be treated as values to fill the

GCM	GWAS Catalog	FinnGen
Ancestry		
broad_ancestral_category	broad_ancestral_category_X	--
country_of_origin	country_of_origin_X	--
country_of_recruitment	country_of_recruitment_X	"Finland"
number_of_individuals	number_of_individuals_X	n_cases + n_controls
ancestry_source_id	study_accession	phenocode
Cohort		
trait_name	mapped_trait	name
case_number_initial	initial_sample_description [MANUAL]	n_cases
control_number_initial	initial_sample_description [MANUAL]	n_controls
individual_number_initial	initial_sample_description [MANUAL]	--
triosNumber_initial	initial_sample_description [MANUAL]	--
case_number_replicate	replication_sample_description [MANUAL]	--
control_number_replicate	replication_sample_description [MANUAL]	--
individual_number_replicate	replication_sample_description [MANUAL]	--
trios_number_replicate	replication_sample_description [MANUAL]	--
cohort_source_id	study_accession	phenocode
Dataset		
name	dataset_name	dataset_name
data_type	"gwas"	"gwas"
format	"gdm"	"gdm"
assembly	"GRCh38"	"GRCh38"
is_annotation	"false"	"false"
Item		
item_source_id	study_accession	phenocode
size	manually_curated__origin_file_size	manually_curated__local_file_size
date	manually_curated__origin_last_modified_date	manually_curated__download_date
checksum	manually_curated__origin_md5	manually_curated__local_md5
platform	platform__snps_passing_qc	--
file_name	study_accession + "gdm"	phenocode + "gdm"
Experiment_type		
technique	genotyping_technology	"FinnGen_technique"
Case_study		
case_source_id	pubmedid	phenocode
source_site	study	"https://www.finngen.fi/en"
path_https	link	externalRef
Project		
program_name	"Gwas Catalog"	"FinnGen"
project_name	"Gwas Catalog"	"FinnGen"

Fig. 2. Attribute mapping from source-specific metadata to Genomic Conceptual Model. In this figure are not reported the items of the *Biological View* since it has no corresponding GWAS metadata.

corresponding GCM attributes. Let us consider the metadata *assembly*; for both the two sources the value "GRCh38" is manually inserted since it is not contained in any of the raw attributes.

Some GCM attributes are obtained by the concatenation of two raw metadata (e.g., *file_name* = *study_accession* + "gdm") or by their sum, if they are numeric (e.g., *number_of_individuals* = *n_cases* + *n_controls*).

The progressive numbers nearby the attributes describing the ancestries of GWAS Catalog refer to the multiple ancestries linked to a single cohort. Let us consider the instance of the GCM proposed in Fig. 3; the item with accession "GCST007269" is linked to the cohort with id "2055", which is linked to two different ancestries (respectively ids "5473" and "5476"). The attributes of these two ancestries, before being mapped, are referred with two different progressive numbers.

ancestry			
Id	cohort_id	category	country
5473	2055	European	NR
5476	2055	Native	U.S.
5480	2056	European	NR
5483	2057	East Asian	China
5484	2058	European	Turkey
5486	2060	NR	Finland
5487	2061	NR	Finland
5488	2062	NR	Finland

cohort		
Id	item_id	trait_name
2055	2054	pulse pressure
2056	2055	diabetes
2057	2056	membranous glomerulonephritis
2058	2057	membranous glomerulonephritis
2060	2059	viral fevers
2061	2060	infectious agents
2062	2061	Helminthiases

item		
item_id	file_name	dataset
2054	GCST007269.gdm	1
2055	GCST009379.gdm	1
2056	GCST010004.gdm	1
2057	GCST010005.gdm	1
2059	AB1_ARTHROPOD.gdm	2
2060	AB1_BACT_BIR.gdm	2
2061	AB1_HELMINTIASES.gdm	2

Fig. 3. An instance of the Genomic Conceptual Model containing four items from GWAS Catalog (light blue) and three items from FinnGen (green). In this figure are reported only the entities corresponding to the *GWAS View*. Moreover, are reported only the relevant attributes to show the proper cardinalities between the entities, the full list of the attributes is reported in Fig. 2. (Color figure online)

The attributes marked with the label "MANUAL" are not reported as they are but need a syntactic transformation. The metadata `initial_sample_description` and `replication_sample_description` are written in plain text: their values are parsed to fill the GCM attributes of the cohort. Here we report the example item extracted from study accession "GCST005538": `initial_sample_description` = 1,726 European ancestry cases, 5,482 European ancestry controls; `replication_sample_description` = 1,912 European ancestry cases, 5,938 European ancestry controls, 781 African American cases, 876 African American controls. As a result of our transformation, the attributes of the corresponding cohort become: CaseNumber_initial = 1726, ControlNumber_initial = 5,482, CaseNumber_replicate = 1,912 + 781, ControlNumber_replicate = 5,938 + 876.

5 The Case of "traitName"

GWAS studies follow the phenotype-first approach: the participants of these studies are classified according to their clinical manifestations. The feature of GWAS studies is to search for SNPs given a phenotype. This is the reason why it is interesting to understand the set of phenotypes present in both the sources considered in this work.

All traits in GWAS Catalog are mapped over the EFO ontology [10]. Traits in the GWAS Catalog are highly diverse and include diseases (e.g., Type II diabetes), disease markers (e.g., measurements of blood glucose concentration), and non-clinical phenotypes (e.g., hair color). The Experimental Factor Ontology was chosen as the ontology to represent GWAS Catalog traits as it is highly adaptable and extensible. It is freely available in OWL format from the EFO website and can be browsed in the Ontology Lookup Service. At the moment of writing (July 2021), the GWAS Catalog contains 2,413 different traits from the EFO ontology. Each study is characterized by one or more traits contained into the source-specific attribute "mapped_trait", comma-separated.

FinnGen phenotypes are instead harmonized over the International Classification of Diseases (ICD) revisions 8, 9 and 10, cancer-specific ICD-O-3, (NOMESCO) procedure codes, Finnish-specific Social Insurance Institute (KELA) drug reimbursement codes and ATC-codes [8]. The latest release at the moment of writing (July 2021) is the fifth one. In its manifest all the files available are listed, each with its corresponding phenotype. The fifth release contains 2803 different phenotypes.

Applying exact string matching between the list of phenotypes of the two sources, 94 traits are found to be shared. More sophisticated semantic matches are subject to future extension of this work [4].

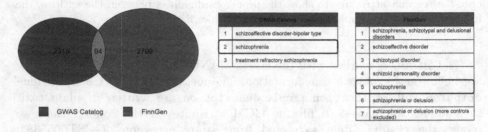

Fig. 4. Left: Intersection of the sets of phenotypes of the two sources GWAS Catalog and FinnGen. The intersection is obtained through exact matching of the two sets and it represents a small portion of both of them. Right: Traits related to "schizophrenia". The blue table reports the phenotypes of GWAS Catalog; the green table is dedicated to FinnGen. Only one trait is shared, all the others require domain experts to be correctly mapped. (Color figure online)

A graphical representation of the intersection of the sets of phenotypes (with exact matching) is provided in Fig. 4. In the same figure, we report an example of the matching between the phenotypes of the two repositories. In both tables we report all the phenotypes resulting by searching for the word "schizophrenia". Only one common phenotype is spotted using exact matching; more correspondences may be found with semantic match (note that mapping phenotypes requires further effort and experts validation).

6   Datasets Interoperability

Using the GenoMetric Query Language (GMQL) [14] many genomic datasets belonging to the GeCo repository can be jointly queried based on the values of some corresponding attributes [15]. The GMQL operators exploit the transformed source-specific attributes and not the original ones, to ease the matching between attributes. The most significant attributes of GWA studies are the names of the phenotypes (attribute *traitName* of the cohort) and the ancestral information of the cohort upon which the studies are based on (attributes *countryOfOrigin* and *countryOfRecruitment* of the ancestry).

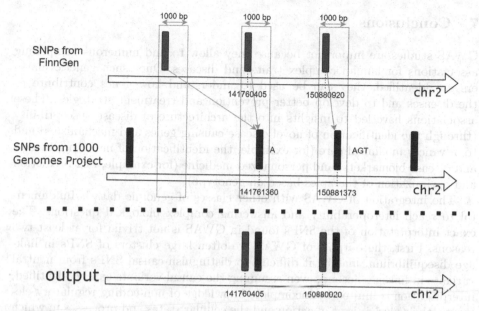

Fig. 5. GMQL query exploiting the integrated datasets FinnGen and 1000 Genomes Project. The query merges the two datasets to extract the couples made of SNPs that are closer than 1000 base pairs. It has been enabled by the META-BASE pipeline and the shared GCM.

Figure 5 graphically represents a query that jointly exploits the FinnGen dataset and the data from 1000 Genomes Project. The genomes sequenced in the 1000 Genomes Projects are not selected with regard to phenotype, so to provide a resource of variants that supports a deeper understanding of newly discovered loci influencing human disease. The projects include SNPs with allele frequencies as low as 1% across the genome and 0.1–0.5% in gene regions, as well as structural variants. It includes genomes from 26 different populations, including the Finnish one.

In the considered query, the SNPs related to the Finnish population are selected from 1000 Genomes, thereby enabling comparisons with the SNPs from FinnGen dataset. From this latter dataset we select only the SNPs which have been found as related to schizophrenia. The goal of the query is to analyze which SNPs of the two datasets are particularly close, specifically within an interval of 1000 base pairs. In the example, only two pairs of SNPs are eventually extracted in the output, as they meet the set distal constraint. Note that the querying of the two initial datasets was only enabled thanks to the integration efforts of metadata and region attributes introduced in this article and building up on [2,3].

7   Conclusions

GWAS studies are important because they allow to find numerous compelling associations for human complex traits and diseases. Once such genetic markers are identified, they can be used to understand how genes contribute to the diseases and to develop better prevention and treatment strategies. These associations have led to insights into the architecture of disease susceptibility (through the identification of novel disease-causing genes and mechanisms) and to advances in clinical care (for example, the identification of new drug targets and disease biomarkers) and personalized medicine (for example, risk prediction and optimization of therapies based on genotype).

The integration of GWAS with other classes of genomic data is fundamental to reach interoperability and answering complex biological questions. The exact interpretation of the SNPs found in GWAS is not trivial for at least two reasons. First, the outputs of GWAS are often large clusters of SNPs in linkage disequilibrium, making it difficult to distinguish causal SNPs from neutral variants in linkage. Second, even assuming the causal variants can be identified, interpretation is limited by incomplete knowledge of non-coding regulatory elements, their mechanisms of action and the cellular states and processes in which they function. For the aforementioned reasons, it is important to further investigate GWAS data by merging different genomic datasets and by performing multi-omic analyses [6].

We started from the GCM, which proposed an integrative schema solution for several genomic repositories. We extended it by adding three entities that are relevant for GWAS and we implemented the data import and transformation pipeline to store the datasets of two new data sources (i.e., GWAS Catalog and FinnGen) within the META-BASE repository. We detailed the mapping effort performed for this purpose and finally demonstrated the usefulness of this work by using a domain-specific language that interrogates FinnGen together with 1000 Genomes datasets for extracting SNPs relevant to the schizophrenia trait.

Acknowledgments. This research is funded by the ERC Advanced Grant 693174 GeCo (data-driven Genomic Computing).

References

1. Bernasconi, A., Canakoglu, A., Masseroli, M., Ceri, S.: The road towards data integration in human genomics: players, steps and interactions. Briefings Bioinform. **22**(1), 30–44 (2021). https://doi.org/10.1093/bib/bbaa080
2. Bernasconi, A., et al.: META-BASE: a novel architecture for large-scale genomic metadata integration. IEEE/ACM Trans. Comput. Biol. Bioinform. (2020). https://doi.org/10.1109/TCBB.2020.2998954
3. Bernasconi, A., Ceri, S., Campi, A., Masseroli, M.: Conceptual modeling for genomics: building an integrated repository of open data. In: Mayr, H.C., Guizzardi, G., Ma, H., Pastor, O. (eds.) ER 2017. LNCS, vol. 10650, pp. 325–339. Springer, Cham (2017). https://doi.org/10.1007/978-3-319-69904-2_26

4. Bernasconi, A., Canakoglu, A., Colombo, A., Ceri, S.: Ontology-driven metadata enrichment for genomic datasets. In: 11th International Conference Semantic Web Applications and Tools for Life Sciences, SWAT4LS 2018, vol. 2275, pp. 1–10 (2018). CEUR-WS
5. Buniello, A., et al.: The NHGRI-EBI GWAS catalog of published genome-wide association studies, targeted arrays and summary statistics 2019. Nucleic Acids Res. **47**(D1), D1005–D1012 (2019)
6. Canakoglu, A., Bernasconi, A., Colombo, A., Masseroli, M., Ceri, S.: GenoSurf: metadata driven semantic search system for integrated genomic datasets. Database **2019**, baz132 (2019). https://doi.org/10.1093/database/baz132
7. Cappelli, E., et al.: OpenGDC: Unifying, Modeling, Integrating cancer genomic data and clinical metadata. Appl. Sci. **10**(18), 6367 (2020)
8. Rambold, G., et al.: Meta-omics data and collection objects (MOD-CO): a conceptual schema and data model for processing sample data in meta-omics research. Database **2019**, baz002 (2019). https://doi.org/10.1093/database/baz002
9. Frankish, A., et al.: GENCODE reference annotation for the human and mouse genomes. Nucleic Acids Res. **47**(D1), D766–D773 (2019)
10. GWAS Catalog Team: GWAS catalog website. https://www.ebi.ac.uk/gwas/
11. International Multiple Sclerosis Genetics Consortium: Multiple sclerosis genomic map implicates peripheral immune cells and microglia in susceptibility. Science **365**(6460), eaav7188 (2019)
12. Kundaje, A., et al.: Integrative analysis of 111 reference human epigenomes. Nature **518**(7539), 317–330 (2015)
13. Masseroli, M., et al.: Modeling and interoperability of heterogeneous genomic big data for integrative processing and querying. Methods **111**, 3–11 (2016)
14. Masseroli, M., et al.: GenoMetric Query Language: a novel approach to large-scale genomic data management. Bioinformatics **31**(12), 1881–1888 (2015)
15. Masseroli, M., et al.: Processing of big heterogeneous genomic datasets for tertiary analysis of Next Generation Sequencing data. Bioinform. **35**(5), 729–736 (2019). https://doi.org/10.1093/bioinformatics/bty688
16. Palacio, A.L., López, Ó.P., Ródenas, J.C.C.: A method to identify relevant genome data: conceptual modeling for the medicine of precision. In: Trujillo, J.C., et al. (eds.) ER 2018. LNCS, vol. 11157, pp. 597–609. Springer, Cham (2018). https://doi.org/10.1007/978-3-030-00847-5_44
17. Pastor, O.: Understanding the human genome: a conceptual modeling-based approach. In: Bringas, P.G., Hameurlain, A., Quirchmayr, G. (eds.) DEXA 2010. LNCS, vol. 6261, pp. 467–469. Springer, Heidelberg (2010). https://doi.org/10.1007/978-3-642-15364-8_38
18. Pastor, O., et al.: Enforcing conceptual modeling to improve the understanding of human genome. In: 2010 Fourth International Conference on Research Challenges in Information Science, pp. 85–92. IEEE (2010)
19. Rambold, G., et al.: Meta-omics data and collection objects (MOD-CO): a conceptual schema and data model for processing sample data in meta-omics research. Database (2019)
20. Reyes Román, J.F., Pastor, Ó., Casamayor, J.C., Valverde, F.: Applying conceptual modeling to better understand the human genome. In: Comyn-Wattiau, I., Tanaka, K., Song, I.-Y., Yamamoto, S., Saeki, M. (eds.) ER 2016. LNCS, vol. 9974, pp. 404–412. Springer, Cham (2016). https://doi.org/10.1007/978-3-319-46397-1_31
21. Rudy, G., Helix, G.: A hitchhiker's guide to next-generation sequencing (2010). http://www.goldenhelix.com/pdfs/whitepapers/Hitchhikers-Guide-to-NGS.pdf

22. Schuster, S.C.: Next-generation sequencing transforms today's biology. Nat. Methods **5**(1), 16–18 (2008)
23. Tam, V., et al.: Benefits and limitations of genome-wide association studies. Nat. Rev. Genet. **20**, 467–484 (2019)
24. The 1000 Genomes Project Consortium: A map of human genome variation from population-scale sequencing. Nature **467**(7319), 1061–1073 (2010)
25. The ENCODE Project Consortium: An integrated encyclopedia of DNA elements in the human genome. Nature **489**(7414), 57–74 (2012)
26. Wang, K., et al.: A genome-wide meta-analysis identifies novel loci associated with schizophrenia and bipolar disorder. Schizophr. Res. **124**(1), 192–199 (2010)
27. Wang, L., et al.: Biostar models of clinical and genomic data for biomedical data warehouse design. Int. J. Bioinform. Res. Appl. **1**(1), 63–80 (2005)
28. Weinstein, J.N., et al.: The cancer genome atlas Pan-Cancer analysis project. Nat. Genet. **45**(10), 1113–1120 (2013)
29. Zheng, R., et al.: Cistrome Data Browser: expanded datasets and new tools for gene regulatory analysis. Nucleic Acids Res. **47**(D1), D729–D735 (2018)

Design of an Adaptable mHealth System Supporting a Psycho-educational Program for Pregnant Women with SGA Foetuses

Sara Balderas-Díaz[1]([✉]) [iD], María José Rodríguez-Fórtiz[2] [iD], José Luis Garrido[2] [iD], Mercedes Bellido-González[3] [iD], and Gabriel Guerrero-Contreras[1] [iD]

[1] Department of Computer Science and Engineering, University of Cádiz, Avda Universidad de Cádiz 10, Puerto Real, 11519 Cádiz, Spain
{sara.balderas,gabriel.guerrero}@uca.es

[2] Software Engineering Department, University of Granada, C/Pdta Daniel Saucedo s/n, 18014 Granada, Spain
{mjfortiz,jgarrido}@ugr.es

[3] Biosanitary Research Institute (Ibs.Granada), Granada, Spain
mmbellid@ugr.es

Abstract. mHealth (mobile Health) systems are turning out very useful in their application to the Life Sciences as they can assist users in several ways by acquiring, storing, visualizing and processing information. These systems consist of hardware and software especially designed to provide required functionalities and properties in order to satisfy stakeholders' needs. This is also of special importance in health as end-users can find in the use of ICTs (Information and Communication Technologies) a key help to address and improve treatment and recovery processes of physical and mental health. This paper presents the design of a mHealth system, which is intended to support a psycho-educational programme devised and supervised by health professionals for pregnant women (and their partners) with SGA (Small for Gestational Age) foetuses. We pay special attention to adaptation and usability properties to tailor the psycho-educational programme and facilitate its use by patients through structured and updated health information and tasks. It tries to avoid obstacles for technology acceptance. As a result, a prototype of the mHealth system has been developed and used by pregnant women and partners in a proof of concept; pregnant women were motivated and informed positive feedback.

Keywords: Pregnant women · SGA foetus · mHealth · Usability · Adaptation

1 Introduction

mHealth (mobile Health) systems [3] can assist health professionals and patients in several ways by acquiring, storing, visualizing and processing information. They exhibit a high potential when providing key functionalities to help in monitoring, diagnosing and treating diseases [19], and active ageing [8]. The success of mHealth systems in

© Springer Nature Switzerland AG 2021
I. Reinhartz-Berger and S. Sadiq (Eds.): ER 2021 Workshops, LNCS 13012, pp. 125–135, 2021.
https://doi.org/10.1007/978-3-030-88358-4_11

clinical environment systems depends on their properties (usability, adaptation, privacy, etc.). A usable and adaptable system increases efficiency and productivity, decreases critical errors, and improves acceptance by the users [15].

In the case of pregnancy, mHealth systems have been used to facilitate the self-report of emotional health (such as depression, anxiety or stress) and wellbeing, and in some cases to motivate changes and to support therapeutic interventions [6]. There are stressors such as fear of pregnancy problems, child malformations, baby care, or change of life. The risk of having a SGA (Small for Gestational Age) or premature baby also increases during pregnancy due to emotional management problems, and currently, the number of cases is increasing worryingly [9]. There is strong evidence that stress during pregnancy causes alterations in the vascular, neuroendocrine and immune systems of the foetus [14], and increases the likelihood of fetal growth retardation and preterm birth [21]. Besides, several studies have demonstrated a relationship between stress of the mother and future mild problems in the offspring, which are manifested from a very early age with low neurobehavioral performance [5] until adolescence with emotional and cognitive problems [1]. Other severe problems could be lower or impaired mental and motor development, or behavior disorders such as attention-deficit and hyperactivity disorder [4, 10]. Prevention, protection and rehabilitation interventions, such as modifying the lifestyle (or enabling a longitudinal monitoring during the pregnancy, should be introduced in order to improve the emotional management and reduce negative consequences [18].

This paper presents the design of an interactive, adaptable mHealth system, which is intended to assist pregnant women (and their partners) with SGA foetuses; it is called mPOP (acronym for **m**Health system assisting **P**regnant w**O**men through a psychoeducational **P**rogramme) system. Its focus is on addressing some important areas such as emotional management, health care, medical advice, and communication with the foetus (for stimulation purposes). The women and their partners can use this programme through an app (mobile application) by carrying out training tasks daily, to put in practice health professionals' indications in a more ecological way (integrated in their daily routine). In the design of the system, we have paid special attention to usability guidelines to increase the users' satisfaction, and to avoid obstacles for the technology acceptance. Besides, the system can be adapted according to specific intervention needs, i.e. psycho-educational programmes can vary in terms of amount and order of tasks, and type and amount of contents.

The paper is structured as follows. Section 2 reviews related work. Section 3 presents the general methodology used to develop this research work. Section 4 characterises the functionality and properties required by users. Section 5 presents the system model and design decisions for the implementation of a mPOP prototype to be used by pregnant women (and partners) in a proof of concept, of which we present preliminary results. Final section summarises conclusions and future work.

2 Related Work

This section introduces related work on mHealth systems in the pregnancy field.

A study was performed by [11], in which participated 410 women who were pregnant or had given birth to at least one child in the past three years. Almost three quarters of respondents had used at least one pregnancy app. The main functionalities of the apps used by the participants for pregnancy were: give useful information 83%; monitoring fetal development 70%; monitoring changes in pregnant woman's body 59%; provide reassurance 58%; facilitate connection with other pregnant women 24%; help keep track of appointments and medical details 16%; share pregnancy information with family/friends 14%; store photos or videos of woman 9%; and store foetal ultrasound images 3%. Many participants complained about the validity of the content of these apps, and their security and privacy aspects.

In [16] a qualitative analysis was performed on two pregnancy mobile applications (Text4Baby and Baby Center's 'My Pregnancy Today'), which are used to query medical information. The latter is the more complete and treats themes such as body and management of pregnancy symptoms, foetal development, prenatal care, maternal well-being, partner roles, etc. Another application for pregnancy (called Bloom) was analysed in [22]. The intervention was focused on tracking and providing customized feedback (daily dashboard) about nutrition, hydration, activity, weight, etc.

The study in [17] evaluated the usability (feasibility and acceptability) and effectiveness of mHealth lifestyle and medical apps to support health care during pregnancy in high-income countries. They review some apps to reduce gestational weight gain by increasing vegetables and fruit intake, to quit smoking cessation, and to support health care for prevention of asthma and infections during pregnancy. The evidence on usability and effectiveness of these apps is limited and needs further investigation before their implementation in health care.

In summary, there are several proposals of applications to monitor the pregnancy. All of them try to provide information to pregnant women to improve their health and self-monitoring. Some of them are usually focused on a single health aspect (e.g. nutrition, depression and diabetes). However, none of them have been created to specifically address the case of pregnant women (and partners) at risk of having SGA through a supervised psycho-educational intervention programme.

3 Methodology

We have adopted a software development-based methodology [20] embracing the following main stages (Fig. 1). Some of them are described in detail in the following subsections/sections. In each stage, some aspects of previous stages were reviewed.

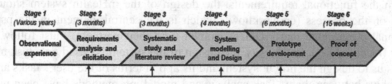

Fig. 1. Methodology stages.

The starting point for this research work comes from an early phase encompassing an observational experience in clinical practice for several years by health professionals (midwives and doctors) at hospitals when assisting women with SGA foetuses in pregnancy control sessions. As the emotional state of pregnant women should be also addressed in daily life, possible benefits of provisioning an intervention programme to be also managed by the women in a more continuous, structured and ecological way.

During a second stage, a research team of professionals in health and computer science identified the more adequate technology (i.e. mHealth systems), by conducting a systematic study on related work and literature review. It led to the third stage intended to analyse and elicit requirements (see Sect. 4) through weekly meetings based on techniques such as: expert interviews and focus groups for quality information collection about stakeholders and organizational settings; and brainstorming for the contribution of new ideas, opportunities and improvements.

The fourth stage was focused on the system modelling and design. The hardware requirements were at least to provide a server computer, and Internet access from the end users' mobile devices. The decision was based on the paradigm called Bring your Own Device (BYOD) [13], where powerful and advanced solutions in eHealth can be developed taking into consideration that users carry their smartphones with Internet connection. On the other hand, the software was built by using several modelling and design techniques. The fifth stage purpose was the iterative development of our operational mPOP prototype (see Sect. 5). It also included a prototype testing in a lab carried out by health professionals. The sixth stage embraced a proof of concept, i.e. a group of mothers and partners with risk of having a SGA baby used the prototype for approximately 15 weeks.

4 Analysis

4.1 Task Model

The functional requirements elicited from the third stage were organized into groups:

- Guide the users in the psycho-educational programme organized in tasks, which should include explanations, instructions/activities, and some questionnaires.
- Access, task accomplishment, and responses to the questionnaires must be monitored to analyse user progress and satisfaction on the programme.
- Analysis of the progress of the pregnancy by health professionals; the mPOP system should allow the programme adaptation for specific interventions.

From the functional requirements, the design of the mHealth system should be focused on the process (or workflow), which is the central element in the psycho-educational programme that pregnant women (and their partners) must follow periodically (ideally daily). In this way, the design of the system is based on a task model. It allows us to design the mPOP system and its app in terms of the user's tasks and the relationships between them. Task analysis and modelling methods have been used to provide a rigorous, structured description of user activity required by the programme to facilitate the design of the system [7].

The task model is implemented as follows. Each task includes sections: a general explanation and activities to be carried out. Each activity is composed of instructions (videos) and questionnaires. Some of the activities provide other multimedia resources such as video and audio (e.g. a song) that should be performed in/under specific places/conditions. The questionnaires collect information related to the progress and manner in which the proposed activities are performed. Besides, some tasks also include an additional "To learn more" section, which offers links to documents with verified information from specialists. Some tasks present activities or instructions that are different for the pregnant woman and her partner.

4.2 Properties

The properties identified for the mPOP system are the following ones:

- Adaptable: Flexibility in the process and contents presented in the form of tasks, in order to better fulfil the needs of learning and practice of methods for pregnancy care. It allows health professionals to easily adapt the psycho-educational programme to specific user's clinical situations (e.g. needs for more tasks addressing stress) and hospital procedures (e.g. shorter programmes).
- Usable: The mHealth system must be user-friendly in order to motivate and engage users in their healthcare in order to guarantee the programme success.
- Reliable: Contrastable, official procedures and contents obtained from reputable sources have to be included and controlled by the health professionals.
- Secure: Health data storing, communication and access have to be secure. For example, the system can be accessed only by authorized users and all the data has to be stored and communicated by using encryption mechanisms. Additionally, data privacy has to be conforming to the regulations. For instance, a user cannot be directly identifiable, i.e. associated with user name.

5   mPOP Design

5.1 System Model

In accordance with the previous requirements analysis, a model for the design of mPOP system has been defined (Fig. 2), it is based on the following entities:

- User data (parents, babies and professonals) from the intervention programme, and data about the programme progress by users are stored in MoSysDB (Monitoring System Database) database (all marked in blue).
- The Vivembarazo mobile application (Vivembarazo App) to access the psycho-educational programme, and a web-based Author Tool for the design of the programme (both marked in green).
- The AdaptEn (Adaptation Engine) module, in charge of implementing the mechanisms for the adaptation in runtime. It follows a component-based design in which different services are injected (marked in yellow).

The participation of the team of health professionals is essential as they design the intervention programme by using the author tool and taking into account the information about woman and partner, the baby is represented in separate entities to provide flexibility and to ensure that the system will be easily extensible. Each programme could have different task structure and organisation of contents, and even different specific contents, and is automatically uploaded by the AdaptEn module when they run the Vivembarazo App. The system is adaptable in terms of: 1) new intervention programmes can be added and the contents of existing ones can be modified; 2) the intervention programme for each pregnant woman can be changed when it is already in progress, for instance, when the healthcare professionals consider other different or additional tasks/activities of those initially planned; and 3) intervention programme can be created in different languages. These three adaptations can be made by healthcare professionals at any time, and no reinstallation is required, as the AdaptEn provides the adaptation functionality to carry changes in runtime. This means that changes within an application will be observable when the users who are using the Vivembarazo App access those tasks and contents next time.

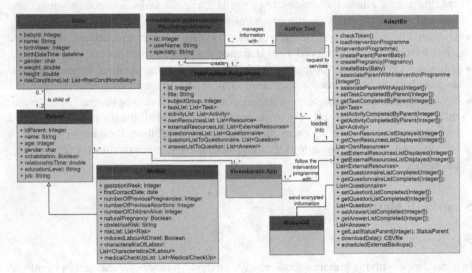

Fig. 2. System model

AdaptEn supports the following actions through the services: (1) automatic load of intervention programmes into the system and their parents association; (2) the inclusion of the elements that compose the intervention programme (task, activities, resources, questionnaires, etc.); and (3) to monitor the degree of performance and completeness of programme by the parents. The AdaptEn services are executed when the healthcare professionals interact with the author tool. Other services are executed when users access the tasks of the intervention programme, visualise the activities within a task or an external/internal resource, and complete a questionnaire. AdaptEn monitors the different contents accessed by the users in the Vivembarazo App, so that each time a user accesses the application, he can continue from its last access state. AdaptEn connects to the external database (MoSysDB) which stores all this information, including multimedia files (videos and audios) and links. AdaptEn includes the downloadData service to download the data selected from MoSysDB, and the scheduledExternalBackups service to schedule backups to external servers.

The proposal follows a multi-layered architecture model. The presentation layer hosts the interface, and the presentation logic for the Vivembarazo App and the Author Tool. The Author Tool is deployed in an external server and accessible by using standard web technologies (i.e. navigators). The AdaptEn module is hosted in a cross-cutting services layer. Clients connect to the server, make a request (HttpRequest) and the response message is encapsulated in an HTTP-response. Security aspects are covered by the checkToken service which establishes a secure connection and encrypts the information transmitted over the network.

5.2 Vivembarazo App

A poor usability in the use of technology decreases user productivity and consequently causes loss of users. Apart from questionnaires to assess usability, well-known usability guidelines can be used in design time to guarantee usable applications. In mPOP, pregnant women and their partners will use the app daily for a few minutes. As they will use their own Android smartphones, the Android Design guidelines [2] have been taken into account to guarantee usability and compatibility between different models. The use of common User Interface (UI) patterns and icons (from Material Design by Google) will ensure also familiarity, without redefinition. Table 1 summarises the main guidelines associated with different usability aspects such as user interface design and navigation, notifications management and presentation of the functionality, as well as security aspects.

Apart from these usability guidelines from Android, we have also considered the Guidelines for Designing Graphical User Interfaces of Mobile E-Health in [12]. Thus our app adapts the interface dimension because it is responsive, presents four screens as maximum (authentication, tasks menu, sections task menu and section), includes scroll-bar and displayable menus, and the navigation is proper and easy, avoiding redundant clicks. In our case, the app includes no chats; therefore some guidelines related to this functionality are not applicable.

According to the general structure of the task model described above, there is an introduction task to present the application and its objectives, and 20 more tasks organized organised in four main pregnancy areas: medical advices, health care, communication with the foetus (stimulation), and emotional management. For example, the medical advices group includes tasks: 3 Midwife (Trim. 1 and 2), 4 Gynecologist (Trim. 1 and 2), 10 Midwife (Trim. 3), etc. The numbers indicate preferable order to be done independently of the group they belong.

Figure 3 shows the menu of tasks, a task including the different sections with several activities, a question in a questionnaire, and a document in a specific "To learn more" section of a task. Most of the tasks contents are multimedia resources.

Table 1. Usability guidelines for the Vivembarazo App

User Interface Design	Navigation	Functionality	Security
Consistent in all screens	Correct navigation order in questionnaires	Audio stops when screen is off	Users identification
Layouts are responsive	Hierarchy of navigation clear: tasks –sections- contents	Just one click to interact	Data encrypted in the database
One column, scrolling one direction	Minimum number of steps to reach a specific functionality: 3 steps in our case	No time limit to read and view contents and to complete questionnaires	All network traffic is sent over SSL and a Network Security Configuration file has been defined to customize the security
Buttons and sections in tasks are finger friendly	Notifications	The app displays graphics, text, images, and other UI elements without distortion, blurring, or pixelation	Request access token has been implemented to ensure that requests received are from authenticated clients
Texts in section "To learn more" are clear, concise, syntactically and orthographically correct. They can be enlarged	Requires permission for notifications, used to ask the users to complete new sessions	No services are running when the app is in the background	The system does not share contents with other applications or systems
Colours used to show changes of state, such as completion of a task	Advertising and content unrelated to the core information is not shown	When returning to the foreground, the app returns the user to the exact state in which it was last used	Fulfillment of the Protection Data Laws

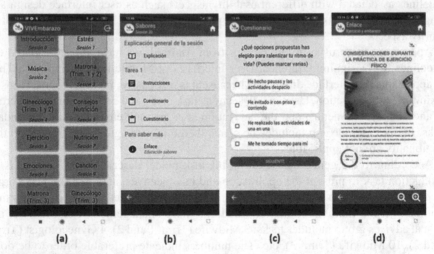

(a)　　　　(b)　　　　(c)　　　　(d)

Fig. 3. (a) Menu of tasks, (b) Sections in a task, (c) Questionnaire, and (d) Document

5.3 Preliminary Results

A prototype of the mPOP system has been developed and used by pregnant women and their partners during a proof of concept. After it, all of them provided positive feedback about its usefulness. In particular, preliminary results (Fig. 4) show that 63.5% of a total of 24 users have completed more than 65% of the programme. Note that some

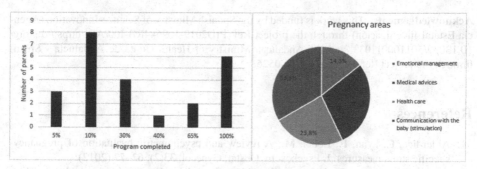

Fig. 4. Parental engagement in the intervention programme (left) and percentage of engagement in the tasks grouped by the four main areas (right).

mothers could abandon the programme before completing it due to the birth of premature babies. Furthermore, it should be highlighted that the areas of greatest interest for the participants were communication with the baby (i.e. stimulation) (33%), followed by medical advices (28.6%).

6 Conclusions and Future Work

This paper presents a case of application of ICT to the health domain by designing a mHealth system (called mPOP), which is intended to assist pregnant women (and partners) with SGA foetuses in training tasks through a psycho-educational programme. The adopted methodology for this research work embraces all the typical stages in a software development life cycle. After the analysis of the mPOP system, we pay special attention to the usability and adaptation properties for a quality design, thus seeking to facilitate the access by users to structured and updated information and tasks of the programme through the Vivembarazo App provided by mPOP system. This design is intended to increase users' satisfaction, and avoids obstacles for technology acceptance. mPOP favours deployment, adapts to different purposes thanks to its flexible structure; therefore it reduces development and maintainability time and cost. A first proof of concept has been carried out with satisfactory results.

Currently, we are planning to extend the psycho-educational programme to the postpartum phase as required by the health professionals. Most of the mothers, partners and newborns need additional assistance and continuity of the programme for one year after the birthday. In this postpartum phase different tasks and contents must be provided to the mothers and partners depending on specific conditions. For instance, some babies can require a period of hospitalization (and others not) for special healthcare and monitoring. The built-in adaptation mechanisms we have endowed to the mPOP system can be enough to extend the programme to postpartum phase. The author tool and the AdaptEn module will allow health professionals to create new tasks with specific contents for it. It should also be validated in the real clinical setting. As additional future work, a detailed usability analysis will be carried out on the basis of the users' answers to several specific questionnaires that have been included in certain tasks of the app Vivembarazo for that purpose.

Acknowledgements. This work is funded by the Spanish Ministry of Science-Innovation (Agencia Estatal Investigación) through the project Ref. PID2019-109644RB-I00/AEI/https://doi.org/10.13039/501100011033, and the Andalusia Ministry of Health (Junta de Andalucía - Spain) through the project Ref. PC-0526-2016-0526.

References

1. Alderdice, F., Lynn, F., Lobel, M.: A review and psychometric evaluation of pregnancy-specific stress measures. J. Psychosom. Obstet. Gynecol. **33**(2), 62–77 (2012)
2. Android Developers: Design & quality (2021). https://developer.android.com/docs/quality-guidelines/core-app-quality
3. Becker, S., Miron-Shatz, T., Schumacher, N., Krocza, J., Diamantidis, C., Albrecht, U.V.: mHealth 2.0: experiences, possibilities, and perspectives. JMIR mHealth uHealth **2**(2), e24 (2014)
4. Bellido-González, M., Díaz-López, M.Á., López-Criado, S., Maldonado-Lozano, J.: Cognitive functioning and academic achievement in children aged 6–8 years, born at term after intrauterine growth restriction and fetal cerebral redistribution. J. Pediatr. Psychol. **42**(3), 345–354 (2017)
5. Bellido-González, M., et al.: Psychological distress and resilience of mothers and fathers with respect to the neurobehavioral performance of small-for-gestational-age newborns. Health Qual. Life Outcomes **17**(1), 1–13 (2019)
6. Doherty, K., Barry, M., Belisario, J.M., Morrison, C., Car, J., Doherty, G.: Personal information and public health: design tensions in sharing and monitoring wellbeing in pregnancy. Int. J. Hum. Comput. Stud. **135**, 102373 (2020)
7. Forrest, E., Bowie, P.: Task analysis. In: Safety and Improvement in Primary Care: The Essential Guide, pp. 56–66. CRC Press (2020)
8. Garcia-Moreno, F.M., Bermudez-Edo, M., Garrido, J.L., Rodríguez-García, E., Pérez-Mármol, J.M., Rodríguez-Fórtiz, M.J.: A microservices e-Health system for ecological frailty assessment using wearables. Sensors **20**(12), 3427 (2020)
9. He, H., et al.: Prevalence of small for gestational age infants in 21 cities in China, 2014–2019. Sci. Rep. **11**(1), 1–10 (2021)
10. King, Z.D., et al.: micro-Stress EMA: a passive sensing framework for detecting in-the-wild stress in pregnant mothers. Proc. ACM Interact. Mob. Wearable Ubiquit. Technol. **3**(3), 1–22 (2019)
11. Lupton, D., Pedersen, S.: An Australian survey of women's use of pregnancy and parenting apps. Women Birth **29**(4), 368–375 (2016)
12. Mendoza-González, R., Rodríguez, F.J.Á., Arteaga, J.M., Mendoza-González, A.: Guidelines for designing graphical user interfaces of mobile e-health communities. In: Proceedings of the 13th International Conference on Interacción Persona-Ordenador, pp. 1–4, October 2012
13. Moyer, J.E.: Managing mobile devices in hospitals: a literature review of BYOD policies and usage. J. Hosp. Librariansh. **13**(3), 197–208 (2013)
14. Nast, I., Bolten, M., Meinlschmidt, G., Hellhammer, D.H.: How to measure prenatal stress? A Systematic Review of Psychometric Instruments to Assess Psychosocial Stress During Pregnancy. Paediatr. Perinat. Epidemiol. **27**(4), 313–322 (2013)
15. Nayebi, F., Desharnais, J.M., Abran, A.: The state of the art of mobile application usability evaluation. In: 2012 25th IEEE Canadian Conference on Electrical and Computer Engineering (CCECE), pp. 1–4. IEEE, April 2012
16. O'donnell, B.E., Lewkowitz, A.K., Vargas, J.E., Zlatnik, M.G.: Examining pregnancy-specific smartphone applications: what are patients being told? J. Perinatol. **36**(10), 802–807 (2016)

17. Overdijkink, S.B., Velu, A.V., Rosman, A.N., Van Beukering, M.D., Kok, M., Steegers-Theunissen, R.P.: The usability and effectiveness of mobile health technology–based lifestyle and medical intervention apps supporting health care during pregnancy: systematic review. JMIR mHealth uHealth **6**(4), e109 (2018)
18. Penders, J., Altini, M., Van Hoof, C., Dy, E.: Wearable sensors for healthier pregnancies. Proc. IEEE **103**(2), 179–191 (2015)
19. Rowland, S.P., Fitzgerald, J.E., Holme, T., Powell, J., McGregor, A.: What is the clinical value of mHealth for patients? NPJ Digit. Med. **3**(1), 1–6 (2020)
20. Ruparelia, N.B.: Software development lifecycle models. ACM SIGSOFT Softw. Eng. Notes **35**(3), 8–13 (2010)
21. Staneva, A., Bogossian, F., Pritchard, M., Wittkowski, A.: The effects of maternal depression, anxiety, and perceived stress during pregnancy on preterm birth: a systematic review. Women Birth **28**(3), 179–193 (2015)
22. Wenger, M.S., Bell, J., McEvoy, P., Yamaguchi, C., Shokrpour, A.: Bloom: fostering healthy and peaceful pregnancies with personal analytics. In: CHI 2014 Extended Abstracts on Human Factors in Computing Systems, pp. 245–250 (2014)

Author Index

Printed in the United States
by Baker & Taylor Publisher Services